Praise For
THE MISUNDERSTOOD GOD

"Darin Hufford has crafted a beautiful narrative that meshes spiritual memoir with biblical exposition. In THE MISUNDERSTOOD GOD he presents a Lord that countless Christians have never met, yet the One Scripture describes as the embodiment of relentless Love. This is a marvelous book."

—Frank Viola, author of *From Eternity to Here*, *Reimagining Church*, and (with George Barna) *Pagan Christianity*

"If you have ever struggled with the schizophrenic, seemingly contradictory notions of how this God of love is often portrayed as an angry taskmaster, full of rules and judgment, THE MISUNDERSTOOD GOD will make refreshing sense out of all the religious nonsense. This book scratches where *The Shack* caused you to itch."

—Brad Cummings, collaborator on *The Shack*

"This book thrusts the reader into an absolute 'no spin' zone. Masks of hypocrisy, pretension, and religious folly are ripped away while exposing the reader to the exhilaration of unmitigated spiritual freedom. This book is reserved for those committed to serious inquiry of truth—others need not apply."

—Raymond E. Meadors, PhD, licensed clinical psychologist, Denver, Colorado

"THE MISUNDERSTOOD GOD will help you draw closer to God, know who you are in God, and as a result enhance every one of your relationships. Don't wait to read this book—it will change every relationship in your life for the better."

—Tim Hallmark, sports performance and fitness trainer

"THE MISUNDERSTOOD GOD is the perfect sister-book to *The Shack*. I carry them together. Darin Hufford shows readers that they've known the truth all along. This book puts into words the things inside my heart that I've felt for over sixty years but couldn't get out. I feel liberated after having read THE MISUNDERSTOOD GOD."

—Clinton R. Davis, Hollywood, California

"*Finally!* A book that tells everything I've always known in my heart about who God is but have never been able to put into words for myself. Chapter by chapter, the weights of rejection, worthlessness, unfulfilled expectations, and bold-faced lies were lifted and replaced with the simple yet powerful truth of who He is—Love—and in that there is security!"

—Heather Van Leuven, Phoenix, Arizona

"I only wish I had this book thirty-five years ago. If I had known, when I was young, about the true love of God maybe I wouldn't have made so many mistakes. It was absolutely like breathing 100 percent pure oxygen for the first time. This book truly shows the actual heart of God. My whole outlook on life has changed since this encounter. I will truly never be the same."

—Jan Cox, Hobbs, New Mexico

"I will definitely be reading this book more than once. As I read it, I found myself reading the same sentence over and over and out loud sometimes because I couldn't help myself! I had to make myself put it down today, I want to be able to really let these things soak in—I totally get it."
—Jana Guild, Phoenix, Arizona

"THE MISUNDERSTOOD GOD gives back life to those who lost it for many years in their Christian walk. Darin Hufford shows the reader the true face and heart of God. He reintroduces us to a Father who loves us and in return we want to love. When you read this book, you will never be the same."
—Heather Bean, Cowboy Junction
Church, Hobbs, New Mexico

"There is not a more insightful and heart-moving book on the love of God than THE MISUNDERSTOOD GOD. This book has influenced the way I look at God, people, and ministry altogether."   —Marion Logan, Honolulu, Hawaii

"I encourage all to read this book. No matter how long you have been a Christian or how deep you feel you are in the ministry, this book will leave you knowing God in an intimate way you never thought possible."
—Carol Martin-Dryden, Sydney, Australia

"Is it possible that buried deep beneath the logic of religion there is a God you have not yet met or experienced? THE MISUNDERSTOOD GOD tells the story of one man, Darin Hufford, who had to unlearn virtually everything he had been taught about God in order to find true spiritual peace and freedom.

"Teilhard de Chardin wrote, 'Someday, after we have mastered the wind, the waves, the tides and gravity, we shall harness for God the energies of love. And then, for the second time in the history of the human race, we will have discovered fire.' Darin Hufford has discovered this fire in THE MISUNDERSTOOD GOD by masterfully unpacking three profound words: *God is love*.

"If you are willing to set aside what you think you already know about God, this may be one of the most important books you'll ever read."

—Jim Palmer, author of *Divine Nobodies* and *Wide Open Spaces*

THE
MISUNDERSTOOD
GOD

The lies religion
tells about God

DARIN HUFFORD

windblown
MEDIA

Adapted from the previously published title *The God's Honest Truth*.

Published by Windblown Media
4680 Calle Norte
Newbury Park, CA 91320
office@windblownmedia.com

Published in association with Hachette Book Group, Inc.
Hachette Book Group
1290 Avenue of the Americas
New York, NY 10104

www.HachetteBookGroup.com

Printed in the United States of America

First Edition: November 2009

10 9 8 7 6

Library of Congress Control Number: 2009924636

ISBN 978-1-935-17005-1

First, to the one who inspires everything I do.
Through my love for my wonderful wife, Angie,
I hear the whispers of God Himself. You are my world
and my life. I love you.

Also, to my four precious daughters Landin, Sidney,
Emma, and Eva, and my son, Jude.
There are simply no words to describe the love I have
for you. You are the total sum of who I am.

Contents

CHAPTER 1

The Lie We Were Told

I f you think there's any good in you, you better hold on for your life because God's about to knock you off your throne and expose the truth of how wicked you really are."

"Amen!" The crowd egged him on, showing their approval by raising their hands as if to say, "It's happened to me, and I liked it!"

"He's not gonna share His glory with you or anyone else!"

"Preach it!" came a voice from somewhere in the front row. I strained to see who it was, but the lady with the beehive hairdo was sitting right in front of me.

"God is God, and the sooner you realize that, the better off you'll be, and if He's got to take one of your children home to get your attention—He'll do it!"

"That's right—yes He will," came another voice, while a few others nodded their heads really big and clapped their hands. This time I didn't have to strain to see who it was because it was the beehive lady herself saying it. Her husband put his big arm around her and pulled the frail, nice-smelling lady close to him as if to protect her and keep her warm at the same time. I sank down in my seat, hoping that no one was looking our way.

The images of the old church that I grew up in have been indelibly etched into my mind. The smell of the sanctuary, the depressed lighting that the sun made through the stained-glass windows, even the texture of the fabric on the pews has been forever stamped into my psyche. I think about it at the oddest times. I'll be driving down the road or shopping in the grocery store, and something will remind me of that time in my life. I didn't like visiting God's house. It was always sad there. It seemed like we were always in trouble. My mother was always *shushing* me no matter what I said. I really hated that. Even when I whispered really quietly she would say, "Shhhhh," like I was being too loud. I really did not like growing up in church, but that's where all our friends were so I figured that's why we did it too.

The God they told me about was not someone I would want to be friends with. I remember thinking how unfortunate it was that we had to "love" Him in order to go to heaven. It reminded me of when Bobby Kendal got the new GI Joe helicopter. Everyone hated Bobby because he was a jerk, but we all acted like we liked him so he'd let us fly our GI Joes around in it. Otherwise we were left to tying them to the back of our bikes and watching them tumble and scrape across the dirt as we rode through the desert. Sometimes that was better anyway. It looked so lifelike when they flipped and fell all over while being towed through rocks and potholes. Especially when accompanied with the moaning and screaming sound effects that every kid had mastered. I always felt like a sellout when I played with Bobby because I didn't want to be there. He knew it and I knew it. It was all about those toys he had. In the end, we all preferred the bike-pull to the helicopter anyway.

Was trying to make God think we liked Him even worth it? How bad could hell be anyway? Was it really as hot as they said? How could they know that for sure? It didn't seem like a very fair choice, if you ask me. If God really wanted to know if we loved Him, why didn't He create two heavens and see whether we'd choose the one with Him in it? Burning for eternity if we didn't choose to go live with Him seemed like a stacked deck. Perhaps He knew we wouldn't choose Him, just as Bobby Kendal knew we wouldn't play with him unless he brought his toys. Whatever the reason, it was obvious to me that God needed a personality makeover if He ever wanted people to play with Him.

I said a "sinner's prayer" when I was seven, and I was baptized a year later. I did both because it seemed to make my mother happy; plus, some of the other kids in our church were doing it. I remember the water was really warm, and it was neat being up in front of everybody. Right before dunking me, the pastor asked me if I loved God. Without hesitation I said, "Jesus," and then smiled at the audience. I knew by then that Jesus was the safe answer to just about any question in church. I said it again, a little confused as to why everyone was chuckling. Then down I went, under the water, and out I came. I was tempted to come up and say "Marco," but I knew my mother would shush me again. They said I was a new person after that, but I felt pretty much the same.

That question, "Do you love God?" started haunting my mind when I got home that night. It wasn't the question that bothered me so much as the answer. My answer was no. I didn't even like Him. I was doing this because I didn't want to go to hell. I was always a bit perplexed as a child when I overheard the adults talking about how much they loved God. *What's there to love?* I thought. He's never satisfied, He wants all the glory, He likes it when we cut ourselves down, He threatens to kill our children, He wants all our money, and He'd light us on fire and feed us to spiders if we didn't give it to Him. What was there to love?

Truthfully, He reminded me of Charlie's dad. Charlie was my best friend in the third grade. His dad was an alcoholic who was unpredictable. One day he'd come home happy and playful, and then at the drop of a hat he would go into a rage and destroy everything in his path. I spent the night at Charlie's house once and then never again. The God I grew up with must have had a drinking problem, I thought. One week the preacher would plead with us in that quivery about-to-cry voice, saying, "Don't you know that God loves you?" and the next week he'd slam his hand down on the podium and tell us, "There's nowhere to hide from the wrath of God." Either God needed to visit the Betty Ford Clinic or something was terribly wrong with our view of Him.

I said the "sinner's prayer" they told me to say, and I did my best to jump through the hoops and follow the rules, but I always felt like I was missing something or like I was always one step behind everyone else in the church. By the time I was twenty-five years old, I was following the picture-perfect Christian path. I did everything they told me to do in order to know God. I read my Bible for hours and hours each day. I spent countless hours praying and calling out to Him. I attended every church service faithfully and gave thousands of dollars in the offering. I even went to Bible college and studied theology.

Eventually I was even hired as a pastor by a well-known megachurch. This was something I had never even dreamed of. I soon began preaching at conferences, churches, and seminars everywhere. I was really good at presenting the gospel, but I was becoming increasingly agitated with my failing religion. In spite of my formula-driven life, I was still empty and unhappy. About a month after I became a pastor, I held my own conference in Phoenix, Arizona.

Losing My Religion

It was the opening evening of my conference. The auditorium began to fill with people who had traveled from all parts of the country. And there was a line at the registration table surrounded by clusters of people wearing nametags and holding conference schedules. Many were from my new congregation. Others had arrived in groups on their church buses.

In a little room behind the curtains on the stage, I sat waiting to go on. I'd often sit in this secluded corner to collect my thoughts and pray beforehand. It also allowed me to watch people. I confess that many times I'd skip singing along in worship just to watch.

As I observed the people, I began to notice there was something familiar about the looks on the faces of this crowd. It was a mix of anticipation and hopeless disappointment. If I had to guess, I'd say it was about 10 percent expectation and 90 percent disappointment. These people were clearly disappointed by something far deeper than the uncomfortable seating and the cheap nametags. This look was something I personally recognized because I saw it in my own eyes every morning while I was standing in front of the mirror.

They had the look of people who'd been sold a religion that didn't work.

They'd been deceived into buying a product that didn't live up to its claims. They were here to find out what went wrong. Why wasn't it working? What part were they missing? Had they misinterpreted the instruction manual? Why didn't it work like the picture showed on the box? Perhaps if they were lucky, they might find that mystery clamp that was supposed to hold everything together at this seminar and a fastener at the next. But history had proven to them that it was very unlikely this conference would be any different than the others they had attended. They stood there, these beautiful people, with laminated nametags, their class schedules, and their hands in the air, trying to be faithful, positive Christians. In their hearts, however, they were skeptically watching another Christian infomercial that would most likely fall short of its exaggerated claims.

The last thing these precious people needed was another sermon full of empty promises and quick-fix formulas. By now, they had heard it all. They'd already tried everything they'd been taught, and they came up empty. It was clear that they had entered the religious world of self-loathing where, rather than question the system, they just blamed themselves to death.

As the worship portion ended, I nervously approached the stage. I'd determined to ask a single question of everyone in the room. It was a question that would change the entire course of my ministry and the lives of many around me. Had I known the mess it would create in so many lives, I might have decided to stay quiet. This one question marked the beginning of a journey and the beginning of the end of my career in the ministry.

I approached the podium. I could see them waiting for me to say something, anything, that would convince them this conference wasn't going to be just another confirmation of their deepest disappointments. After asking them to be completely honest while they bowed their heads and closed their eyes, I cleared my throat and asked,

"How many of you are afraid of the Rapture?"

I stepped back from the microphone to scan the quiet auditorium. My heart almost stopped. To my great horror and amazement, *almost every hand in the building went up.*

Now, allow me to inform you that this was not a group of baby Christians who needed a little more guidance and encouragement in their spiritual journeys. These people were the active heart of their churches. Many were pastors, deacons, children's workers, and leaders of prayer teams and Sunday school classes who had come with their groups. Many people from my own congregation were there as well, and the majority were people who grew up in church.

My next question picked up whoever wasn't taken in by the first question. I asked, "How many of you feel you've basically been miserable for the largest part of your Christian life?"

It was a large auditorium, so I can't be sure. But I couldn't see a single person in that building without their hand up! Imagine. Every Christian present admitted he or she was afraid of the return of Jesus Christ and basically miserable. The very thing I had suspected from childhood about the religion I'd grown up in was about to be confirmed.

For the next hour of our conference, we started down a path of total honesty. We began to frankly ask questions that had been begging for answers the majority of our Christian lives. I'm talking about those questions that would make you feel almost pagan if you were to voice them aloud. Those secret questions that Christians wouldn't dare admit they have, because doing so would almost certainly be misconstrued as faithlessness. We trod through all of those questions and came up with a conclusion that was both startling and simple. Maybe we weren't the first ones to discover this, but we may have been the first Christians to recognize it and not lose our faith because of it. Our conclusion that day was:

We have been lied to about God.

Who He is, what He is like, what He wants from us, and how He relates to us. How He responds to us, what He expects from us, His heart for us, His purpose for us, His desires, and, most of all, His love for us. About all of these things, we'd accepted contradicting lies that simply didn't add up. The terrifying fact is that God's true heart is basically unknown by many of the very people who claim to know Him best. And yet, somehow we had all believed the lies. We weren't going through and replacing our skewed theology point by point with the real truth. In fact, we weren't even claiming to know the truth. On this particular day our revelation was one of common sense. The things we had been taught simply did not add up. They couldn't be right because they contradicted themselves at every point.

We weren't gloating over this realization. In fact, we felt foolish. We felt like the woman who suddenly finds out her husband has been cheating on her for years with her best friend.

How could we have missed it?

I suppose every Christian plays his or her part in keeping the lie covered and alive. We do it by lying to others and ourselves about things like our faith, our victory, and our passion. We learn the lingo so we'll fit in with the crowd, and then we just go with the flow. We follow the religious rules of political correctness and keep our questions to ourselves—because questions can appear rebellious.

Maybe it's a matter of peer pressure for most of us. Who wants to face the obvious comebacks we are sure to get if we ask why it's not working? You know what I'm talking about. The "stock" Christian answers we get when people don't know what else to say. "You need to be in the Word," or "You must have secret sin in your life," or "You just need to spend more time in prayer," or the ever-popular "You just need to give it to God." These comebacks all imply personal failure or a lack of commitment. They are designed to shut you up so you won't be tempted to ask confrontational questions that the people who say them don't have the answers to.

We have been lied to about God.

I'm not suggesting that our church leaders met secretly and concocted these lies in order to suffocate us spiritually. I'm simply stating that over the course of years, we have veered away from truth and swallowed lies.

I would like to give you the first accurate prediction concerning the timing of Christ's return that will actually prove to be right. There are thousands of authors and preachers who have tried to predict the timing of the Second Coming, and so far, all of them have been wrong. My prediction will be the first to come true: Jesus Christ is not returning anytime soon!

Imagine being a groom on your wedding day, and just before you go out to meet your bride, someone comes to you and informs you that they found her hiding in a broom closet in absolute terror of your coming. Would you want to come to that? There is no doubt in my mind that until we get a right revelation of who God is, Jesus Christ will not be coming. He wants His bride to rejoice at the trumpet sound, not scream in terror.

Something must be clearly wrong with how we see our God if this is how the majority of Christians think. What is supposed to be the most beautiful day of all to Christians has been used against us to the point where we now live in fear of its arrival.

We have been lied to about God.

I can sit through two hours of Christian television and watch six sermons in a row. Each sermon directly contradicts the others, and no one even questions it. An evangelist will come to our church and preach a sermon on how God will never leave us or forsake us, and sixty seconds later he follows up with an insinuation that He just might. We listen to teachings on God's promises and how they are a free gift, followed by a list of things we must do in order to earn them.

There are between thirty and forty thousand different Christian denominations, each contradicting the others in some
way. Logic alone would dictate that it is next to impossible to
know God by way of church teachings.

Our religion today, with its promises and testimonies,
reminds me of a group of grandmothers exchanging their lat-
est old wives' tales and swearing by them to their dying day.
With each generation the tale gets a little more embellished
and exaggerated, until finally we are left with a religion that
bears no resemblance to the truth and teachings that tell
about a God who never existed.

I am quickly coming to believe that this is the first time
in history that people outside the church have shown more
signs of knowing God's heart than do the people within the
church. People in the world shake their heads in disgust at
the things we teach about God. They know we're wrong, but
for some reason the majority of Christians don't see it. I have
found that the common bar dweller knows more about the
true heart of God than the dedicated churchgoer.

Christians think they know God because they read about
Him in a book. We've been taught that the more we read
the Bible, the more we will know Him. The Pharisees knew
Scripture like the back of their hands, but when God stood
right in front of them, they didn't know Him from Adam.

Relationship with God to this generation of Christianity
is all about reading the Bible. In fact, we believe this so much
that we have even exchanged God for the Bible, attributing all the attributes of God Himself to it. If we don't read it
excessively or understand it, we feel lost and unspiritual. We
feel a million miles from God.

We have been lied to about God.

I once heard that the definition of insanity is when a
person does the same thing over and over expecting differ-

ent results. I have often wondered if religion has the power to take people's sanity. We are constantly taught to deny the truth about the results and believe that something else will take place the next time around. The things we put our faith in and preach to the world are clearly not working, yet we continue to act and talk as if they are. We tithe 10 percent of our incomes and when the recession comes, we see just as many religious people go bankrupt as people who are unreligious. We say, "A family that prays together stays together," and yet some research indicates the divorce rate is actually higher in the church than it is in the rest of the world (see "U.S. Divorce Rates" at www.religioustolerance.org). We claim to have power and peace and joy and spiritual understanding, but in the end, it seems a similar number of people in the church are on medication for depression, anxiety, ADHD, and a host of other emotional problems.

I believe the heart of God is broken over His children's lack of knowledge of who He is. Not angry or vengeful, but simply broken. Imagine having the very one who was supposed to know you better than anyone in the world not even know your name. That is precisely how God feels with this generation.

My desire is to bring not condemnation but freedom to the body of Christ. I do not believe that the answer is to pray for power or fire from heaven to make it all go away. The answer is quite simple: *we need truth!*

This book is a quest for that truth. There can be only one truth, and when it is found it will *not* contradict itself or confuse our understanding of God, but it will reveal the simplicity of who He is. I have come to realize one thing in my many years of church attendance: anytime a preacher reveals a new and deeply profound truth about God that you haven't already considered in your heart, it's probably not true. If

Jesus was serious when He said that the truth was revealed to little children but hidden from the wise and learned, I have to believe that this generation has missed it altogether.

Our religious quest for truth is like a movie I once saw where a gentleman was taking a vision test. He was asked to cover his left eye and read the top row of letters on the chart that was hanging twenty feet away. To the doctor's amazement, the man read the copyright date that was typed in tiny little letters at the bottom right side of the chart. I thought to myself, *Impressive, but he failed the test.* This is the problem with finding the truth about God's heart. Too many of us are looking so deep that we miss the obvious. Unfortunately, many people would rather gratify themselves with deep thinking and extravagant imaginations than accept anything simple and obvious. To these people, truth is a letdown, and this book will frustrate them to death. Remember that Jesus Christ seemed shallow and frustrating to the Pharisees two thousand years ago.

It is my goal not to impress you with something deeper than you have ever imagined, but to show you the "top row of letters" on the chart. I want you to laugh out loud when you read this book while thinking, *Of course! How could I have missed it?* For the most part, I believe that when you read this book, you will feel the way you do when you are frantically tearing your house apart looking for a pencil, only to find that one's resting behind your ear.

In my conference that day, we discovered through simple honesty that the things we'd been told about God just didn't add up. We all knew that our perceptions of Him were grossly skewed and twisted because of our religious upbringing, and we knew that something needed to happen, but what?

CHAPTER 2

Who Is He Really?

I sat quietly in my tiny new office one night looking over
the carvings and scratches in the old Formica-topped desk
and feeling depressed. I could not shake that look I'd seen
in the people's eyes several weeks earlier at the conference. I
couldn't shake the fact that many of those people were part
of my congregation. What had I gotten myself into? I now had
a congregation of people who were spiritually miserable and
weren't afraid to admit it. I knew something needed to be
done, but what? I wished for a moment that I hadn't accepted
the job of pastor. I never wanted it in the first place. I was just
as miserable and let down with my belief system as they were.

I worried that it was only a matter of time before I became
like all the other pastors I'd seen. I feared this more than
anything. Would I begin to beg for money and bore the heck
out of everyone? Would I suddenly be against all drinking
and smoking? Would I start talking in King James Version,
become obnoxiously judgmental and have a secret porn
addiction? All of these things weighed heavily on my mind.

I had been to Bible college, and I'd studied the Scriptures
more than most people I knew. One thing I had going for
me was that I had studied hard and learned everything I
could about God. I was able to hold my own in any Christian conversation. I had learned the Christian lingo and I

spoke it fluently. Because I'd memorized so much of the Bible, I knew the stock answers to what God would do in almost any situation.

The following week, I announced to the people in my group that I wanted to personally meet with everyone in the congregation for one hour. I sent around a scheduling sheet and had each person fill in what time he or she could come into my office. I decided to work on both my days off, and for the next three to four months, I had eight one-hour meetings a day until I'd talked with every single person who would meet with me. My purpose was to get inside their hearts and minds and really connect with them. And I felt I needed to know their names and their stories before I could ever stand in front of them and preach to them.

I didn't interview them or ask them a series of questions in an effort to locate the problem. There was no survey for them to fill out describing their likes and dislikes about the church service. I just sat with them. I listened to them. I looked into their eyes and opened my heart. In the midst of these meetings, something happened that changed my life forever. Something so mesmerizing and beautiful that the moment it came into being, I could see everything with absolute clarity. This was the granddaddy of all great revelations, and I knew for certain that I was one of the first ones to receive it. It changed my entire theology in an instant and made it come alive in a way I had never imagined. Little did I know at the time that what happened to me would ultimately be the beginning of the end of my ministry career. What happened?

I *fell in love* with the people!

It would be so easy to read those words and miss how incredible this was. So let me emphasize what I'm telling you:

I fell absolutely head over heels in love with these people. I'm talking a little-hearts-coming-out-of-my-head-every-time-I-saw-them kind of love. The Hallmark kind that cheesy cards and sappy songs are made of. I loved these people with every fiber of my being. They became as precious to me as my own children. I went to sleep at night thinking of them and awoke in the morning excited to see them again. When any of them called my office, my heart would leap in my chest and I'd feel like a misty-eyed schoolgirl. I'd light up the moment one of them entered the room. They became my reason for life, the only thing that ever mattered.

Now you have to understand that my entire life, I'd loved the message of the gospel more than anything in the world, even more than I loved people. But something changed in me after I fell in love with these people. That moment, the message sprang to life in me and became more beautiful and more powerful than ever before. The heart and appearance of it changed entirely. I could suddenly see that after hundreds of years of preachers' putting the message before the people, it had mutated into something so repulsive and terrible that it actually hurt people rather than helped them. But when I finally loved the people more than the message, I could see exactly what the problem was. In fact, I'm convinced to this day that the only way to know the heart of the pure, unadulterated gospel is through loving the people the message is for.

I've found that when you love people with every part of yourself, you actually see inside their hearts. You become extremely sensitive to every part of their souls as if they were your own. When things are spoken to them, you can see inside them and hear through their ears, see through their eyes, and understand things from their perspective. If someone says something negative to people you love, you can interpret what they heard, how they took it, and what feelings it gave them. It's not as though you see it from a distance or from the outside looking in. You actually experience it with them. Your heart is woven tightly to theirs. When they become the objects of your affection, you suddenly become one with them. Real love takes you outside yourself and allows you to enter and meld with other people's hearts. When they laugh, your heart laughs because you are one. This is the result of love.

Once my eyes were opened to this amazing truth, I suddenly remembered a wedding I attended years before where the pastor read the popular Bible passage that you always hear at weddings. You know the one; it's from 1 Corinthians 13, the "Love Chapter." Every person living in America has heard it at least once:

> Love is patient, love is kind. It does not envy, it does not boast, it is not proud. It is not rude, it is not self-seeking, it is not easily angered, and it keeps no record of wrongs. Love does not delight in evil but rejoices with the truth. It always protects, always trusts, always hopes, always perseveres. (vv. 4–7 NIV)

When read at a wedding, those verses have a romantic sound. I don't think anyone in the audience at these occasions really believes a word of the passage. It's just something you read at weddings, like you read "'Twas the Night Before Christmas" on Christmas Eve. It sounds so pretty when you hear it, but it's not realistic. At this same wedding, I saw a bumper sticker that read "God is love." That made me laugh out loud. *If that were true,* I thought, *it would mean that the entire Christian religion is wrong.* At least everything I grew up hearing. I don't think the outwardly religious could survive such a revelation, much less admit to it. Nevertheless, it did cause me to wonder.

Almost ten years later, I came face-to-face with the revelation of that wedding verse and that bumper sticker. It finally made sense to me. I could suddenly see as clear as a bell what the problem was with most of American Christianity. I knew that we had been lied to about God, but now, for the first time in my life, I was beginning to realize what the actual truth was and how we lost it.

What Has Happened?

I've found that people instinctively know that God is love. It's written on their hearts. Something inside every one of us knows the truth about our Creator. We define God by what we think love is. Sadly, this world has altered the true meaning of love in our minds, and in doing so it has effectively redefined the heart of God to an entire generation.

This wedding passage contains a list of fifteen statements about love. The Bible says, "God is love." This would mean that these fifteen statements are a description of the character and personality of God Himself. You might have even heard this particular passage read with the word *God* replacing the word *love*. If you haven't, I would encourage you to read it that way now because it's very moving.

We can also come to the conclusion that what we believe in our hearts about love is exactly what we believe in our hearts about God. This is precisely where I want to park for a moment. What do you believe about love in your heart? The problem is that the world has taught you that love is the exact opposite of everything written in this passage. Think about it for a moment. I would like to propose to you the idea that you have bought into the world's definition of love, and somewhere in your heart you believe it.

We've been taught that love isn't patient. In fact, we believe that if it's really "love," there is no need to slow things down in a relationship. We don't think love is kind. Most of us attribute pain and hurt to love because we think it's anything *but* kind.

Our passage also says that "love is not self-seeking." This is precisely the opposite of everything the world has raised us to believe. How about the phrase "Love keeps no record of wrongs"? Do I need to elaborate on that one? Then our Scripture tells us that "love always trusts." We have been taught to look at trusting people as if they were foolish and stupid. How about when it says, "Love always perseveres"? With a divorce rate as high as it is today, I think we can pretty much toss that one aside. We have come to believe that people "just grow apart," and "nothing lasts forever." These excuses even have a ring of wisdom when you hear people use them for their failed marriages.

The point I want to make to you is that the world has convinced us that love is the exact opposite of everything listed in that passage. Also I want to make the point that we have bought this lie hook, line, and sinker. Maybe not in our heads, but we have in our hearts.

I want you to make a mental list of how many times you have been hurt by love in your past, whether by someone with whom you were in a romantic relationship or by a member of your immediate family. Take a moment and count.

If you're like most people, you may have several unforgettable instances that have already surfaced in your mind. Now I have a revelation for you: it wasn't love that hurt you! What you were hurt by was the opposite of love, but *in your heart* you believed it was love. Make no mistake about it: love has never hurt you. You were hurt by a deceptive and upside-down definition of love that you swallowed into your heart and believed.

If the Bible says that "God is love" and everything listed in this verse is a description of the character and personality of God, then I have another question: whose description is the *opposite* of everything listed here? The devil.

Let's go a step further. If you believe in your heart that "love" is the opposite of what the Bible says, you will inevitably attribute the character and personality of the devil to God. Think about this for a moment and let it sink in. I believe this is precisely what the vast majority of us believe in our hearts today about God. We basically believe He has the character and personality of the devil.

If Jesus Christ were walking the earth today in human form, I believe His message would be the same to us as it was to the Pharisees of His time: "You belong to your father, the devil." This is precisely the point He was making two thousand years ago. The Pharisees and religious teachers had painted a picture of God that made Him look like Satan himself. They had made it impossible for the people to have a relationship with God simply because they were terrified and repulsed by Him. We are no different today.

On September 11, 2001, two airplanes loaded with hundreds of innocent passengers were hijacked and flown into the twin towers of the World Trade Center. As millions of Americans watched helplessly in their homes, the towers crumbled to the ground, killing thousands of terrified people. Shortly after this event, several of the nation's most influential Christian leaders appeared on national television and publicly declared that *this was God* sending judgment on America for its many sins. They were not alone in this thinking. Hundreds of other Christians followed them in this belief.

During the beginning of the AIDS epidemic, it was quite common to hear our nation's pastors explain that this was a plague sent by God to punish the homosexuals. Many people still hold to this way of thinking today.

Every bad thing that happens in this world gets blamed upon God. If we lose our jobs, we think God is at the root of it. If we have heart attacks, God gave them to us. If we lose loved ones, it's because God killed them. If our businesses fail, we immediately suspect that God is punishing us for something we did. Every terrible thing that happens is charged to God's account. We truly believe that God has the character and personality of the devil.

Just listen to the way we talk about our God. It's no wonder Christians have little interest in reading their Bibles. Who would want to read "His" book? People decide beforehand what their interpretation of Scripture will be. If you think God is angry, the Bible will sound *only* angry to you. If you think He is a drill sergeant, the Bible will come across that way. If you have decided He is disappointed with you, you will see only disappointment in the words of the Bible.

This is why most Christians never read their Bibles! It is natural for us to avoid contact with someone we don't love. Could you imagine if I had to have a support group of men to keep me accountable in the matter of reading my wife's letters to me? If my wife writes me a love letter, I will plow through an army of men to get to that letter just to see what it says. Then I will read it over and over until the paper literally falls apart in my hands.

Our feelings about God are why most Christians don't pray more than five minutes a week. Who would want to talk to Him? I believe that because of the lies we have been told about the heart of God, it is virtually impossible for us to truly love Him. He is terrifying. He turns His face from us.

He removes His hand of protection from us. He causes bad things to happen in our lives. He's just not lovable.

Often when we use terms like "committed to Christ" it's proof that we don't love Him. A commitment is a way of forcing ourselves to do what we don't want to do. This is not what love is. God is *not* looking for Christians to make another commitment. If you have to force it, it's not there. Truthfully, I think that many "committed" Christians need to be "committed" to a psychiatric ward. If it were not for the promise of heaven at the end of their lives, I honestly think they would have been better off unsaved. Religion has rendered them certifiably insane. It has caused some people to surrender every bit of common sense to a series of jumbled and mixed-up teachings that have no rhyme or reason.

We are terrified of Him, and rightly so, because He is just waiting for us to make a mistake or fall into sin so He can blast us into hell. Most of what we do in our religion is based on fear. We give the offering because we truly believe He won't bless us if we don't. We try our best to witness to others about this wonderful and loving Jesus Christ, but in our hearts we don't believe a word of what we're saying. We go through every religious ritual we know in an effort to gain His favor. Our prayer lives have been reduced to confessions of "Forgive me" and "I'm sorry" at the end of the day. Something needs to change and soon.

Our problem today is that we subscribe to a theology we can't trust as far as we can throw it. Can you imagine me telling my wife that I love her and I will never leave her or forsake her, but if she ever cheats on me, I will proceed to torture her for all eternity? Though she may never cheat on me, she will certainly never get close to me. She will do whatever it takes to survive the relationship, but I will *never* have her heart. This is exactly what many Christians believe about their Father.

When I watch Christians go to "gay pride" parades with megaphones and "You're Going to Hell" signs or hatefully picket abortion clinics and heap truckloads of condemnation on the poor women who go to them, I sit in total amazement. Yet what's happening is quite natural. These people are being conformed to the image of their Father. It makes perfect sense: if we believe in our hearts that God has the temperament and disposition of Satan, our character will inevitably be conformed to that image.

When you look at it this way, everything begins to make sense.

More than anything, it makes sense that our religion keeps dying on us. Christianity has become like the old pickup I used to own. It was a classic and definitely authentic-looking, but it broke down every hundred miles and needed to be revived. The word *revival* is not even in the Bible. It was never the intention of God to have a religion that routinely suffered from heart failure. Sadly, we have become addicted to the electrical shock God has to routinely use to bring our religion back to life every hundred years or so.

I've found that if you take every cliché in the Christian world that hurts people, and hold them up to the light of real love, they prove to be repulsive and untrue. The problem is that most people don't have the guts to hold their belief system up to the light of love. They're not even sure they are allowed to. They secretly wonder if doing so might make God feel the way we do when the cashier at the convenience store holds our twenty-dollar bill up to the light. It's a feeling of being accused of counterfeiting and interrogated undeservingly. But holding Christian teachings up to the light isn't in any way mistrusting God. He is the light! If you're a lover of people, you may find that many things you hear from the pulpit Sunday morning don't pass the light-test.

I believe we've been deceived into believing a lie concerning love. But I also believe there's an even deeper place in our hearts that knows exactly what love is. It's a place that many of us have been afraid to trust most of our lives. This is the place I'm hoping you'll go with me in reading this book. I believe everything you read here will be a confirmation of what you already know in your heart.

Could you imagine me holding my nine-month-old son, Jude, in my arms and telling him that under no circumstances would I share my glory with him? What if I lovingly told him that if he disobeyed me again and again, I would pour gasoline on him and light him on fire? What kind of father would I be if I explained to him that he needed to give me 10 percent of everything he had or I would withdraw my hand of protection from his life and allow the fires of hell to swallow him? What if I told one of my daughters that she was put here on this earth to be a servant and a slave to me? Could you picture me telling my children that I've written everything about me down in a book and unless they read it every day of their lives, they'll never know me? What parent would purposely inject their child with a terrible disease as a punishment for disobedience? What father would turn his head away from his son or daughter the moment the child made a mistake?

Come with me on a journey—a journey to the heart of God. I would like to take you through this amazing passage. I'd like to show you something that could change everything for you. I want to invite you into your own heart and show you what already exists there.

If you're ready, open your heart and turn the page.

CHAPTER 3

The Hair-Trigger God?

I was winning, four to zero, when the visibly frustrated doctor began to reset the game board for another round of Candy Land. Even at eight years old, I was snickering to myself because I knew why I was there. The irony has caused me to chuckle to this day. My parents had taken me to a child psychologist because I struggled with severe depression and uncontrollable anger. Among other things, I would blow my temper if I lost at a board game with one of my brothers or sisters. Losing a game pulled some kind of anger trigger within me and I lost control. I have murdered every character in Clue, and I did it in the living room with the tennis shoe. I hated losing!

That is why, on a lovely summer day in the air-conditioned office of Dr. Steel, while sitting Indian-style on his retro-'70s shag carpet, just beneath his "credential wall," I giggled to myself. For some strange reason, I kept winning. In fact, I don't think I've ever experienced a winning streak like that before or since. I wasn't a stupid little boy. I knew why we were playing Candy Land at 10:00 a.m. on a Wednesday. He wanted me to lose so he could witness for himself the exploding boy-volcano my parents had told him about. He wanted me to lose so he could observe the fireworks and then be the hero who would talk me down from the ledge of anger. Little Darin easily lost his patience in life, and the good Dr. Steel had been commissioned to help him find it. Hundreds and thousands of dollars in education, years of studying for exams and researching a final thesis, and it all came down to winning a simple game of Candy Land with an eight-year-old boy. But he couldn't do it. The cards were not in his favor. It was not to be for Dr. Steel.

"I win again!" I cheered. "That's five in a row." Dr. Steel began to show signs of stress and aggravation through his heavily guarded demeanor. *Maybe he should hold his breath and count to ten,* I thought. I imagined him throwing the board across the room and tearing the heads off the little game pieces in a fit of rage. It was becoming increasingly difficult to maintain my composure, as my gingerbread man rounded the final turn before merrily hopping to the finish line for my sixth win in a row. I could feel the tension building, as I made certain to count extra-loudly while skipping the figure from square to square. "You don't need to count out loud," he snarled.

I knew that Candy Land was a game of luck. I knew because I had played this game with my siblings a thousand times. I knew because I had a vague understanding of mathematical principles. But mostly I knew because Dr. Steel kept reminding me every time I won. It was all I could do to hold my eight-year-old self back from rolling all over the Candy Land board, screaming, "Victory!" over and over. But I refrained because I knew that just beyond his office door, my parents sat hopefully in the waiting room, clenching a folded check for $150 made payable to the good doctor for his expertise in teaching patience to little boys. When our session ended, it must have looked like he had earned his money, because out popped a bouncing, joyful eight-year-old followed by an angry psychologist. My parents were not sure what had taken place in that office that day, but they were delighted to see the sparkle return to their child's eyes, even if it was just for one day.

The truth is, I wouldn't have blown my temper if I had lost to Dr. Steel that day. I knew ahead of time what he was looking for. I was even hoping to lose a game just once so I could conduct myself with dignity and charm. I would have proven them wrong. I wouldn't have lost my patience because I knew the end of the story. I understood why we were playing the game. But Dr. Steel wasn't prepared for an extended losing streak. His plan backfired and without recognizing it, he became the impatient one. I have laughed about that experience for almost thirty-five years.

Believe it or not, Dr. Steel did teach me about patience that day. I learned that when you can see the *heart* of something, you will not become so easily stressed or angry at the things that surround it. It's the lack of knowledge that causes you to become impatient.

I think most people see patience as little more than holding back anger. I know my parents did, and I'm pretty sure Dr. Steel did too. If I lost a game and got angry, I was told to hold my breath and count to ten until the anger subsided. Not giving in to that anger is many people's idea of patience. This mind-set requires anger to be present before patience can exist. And while holding back anger is a good thing, it is not the equivalent of having patience. It is in fact the opposite. Sadly, today when we say, "Love is patient," many of us interpret it to mean that love is really angry but it holds back from releasing that anger. As a result of this skewed thinking, many have swallowed the notion that impatience is a characteristic of love.

I have found that few people believe love is patient. In fact, this generation tends to believe that if it's true love, it will throw off all patience. We've come to expect the absence of any sort of patience in the midst of a "real" burning love.

When I was a pastor, I found myself spending much of my time trying to convince new couples to slow down and be patient. They thought they'd found true love, and they were impatient to get married. Others would go to bed together almost immediately. They would tell me their lack of patience was a sign that they were really in love. They actually defined their love by the absence of patience.

Today, anyone who waits longer than four to six weeks in a relationship to have sex may be accused of not caring for his or her partner. Love has been redefined in our hearts. Sadly, we have learned to measure love by how impatient we are in the midst of it. If we really love someone with all our hearts, for many that's a call to skip the foundation-building and go straight to the consummation. We see love as a call to abandon our patience altogether.

Because of this, people tend to redefine God's heart accordingly. I see evidence of a belief in impatient love woven into many Christian teachings as well.

I once heard a preacher say that if we keep making the same mistakes in life, God will finally get to a point where He will lose patience with us, and He'll teach us a lesson we won't soon forget. I am not sure what was more heartbreaking: hearing him say something so heartless, or listening to the wave of amens he received. If this is true about God, we're all in a heap of trouble.

The God many have been raised to fear is extremely impatient. He expects perfection and is impatient with us to get it right. In my home church the possibility of being sent to hell for all eternity was held over my head. It was the other side of God's patience, the fire in the volcano. It seemed as though He *wanted* to send me to hell, and anytime I messed up, He loved the justification for venting His anger.

Of the hundreds of people who have sat in my office for spiritual counseling, I've found that the majority share the same feelings about the state of their relationship with God. They believe in their hearts that God is so disgusted with the way they are living that He can hardly stand it. But He has held back from dishing out what they deserve because He's still a nice guy, even if He has had it with us. It's upsetting to see so many people thinking this way about Him. What's even more disheartening is that many of us have been conformed to the image of what we believe Him to be.

Many churches have taken on this idea of impatient, "tough" love, doing what they believe their Father does. If people don't measure up, the church reminds them of the burning hell awaiting them. This type of church becomes a perfect breeding ground for fakeness where people close their hearts off to others and put on masks to hide from judgment.

My heart grieves when I hear preachers suggesting that God might abandon us if we mess up one too many times. Bible teachers can systematically match sins with particular verses that, taken by themselves, seem to promise hell and damnation if a person died while committing one of these sins. Some preachers have become experts in finding these verses and delivering them to their flocks like spiritual hand grenades. They sow fear and an image of God as being impatient and ready to judge us the moment we make a mistake.

The fact is, this idea of God disregards His sovereignty. It suggests that He has no control over when we die. If He could extend our lives for the sake of saving our souls, wouldn't He do that? Most modern-day churches have painted a picture of a God who watches from a distance and has limited personal involvement. We've come to believe that He's liable to barge in on us in an embarrassing sinful episode and humiliate us. Rules are rules, after all. We were warned to be ready. The bus leaves when it leaves.

Is it any wonder that so many people, including Christians, fear death? Actually, it's not necessarily death itself that scares us, but the timing of our death that makes us nervous. It could happen at the worst possible time. When the music stops, you'd better have a seat picked out or you lose. What's worse is that the Person in charge of the music has no regard for where you're standing when He cuts it short. It's almost as if He wants you to lose.

It is impossible to have patience with someone when you ultimately want to send that person to hell. I know this sounds a bit harsh, but many Christians have been conformed to the image of what they believe exists in God's heart. They are quick to send others to hell and because of that, they have little or no patience with other people's struggles. They have no patience because they don't have love.

I was recently asked to speak to a group of about one hundred pastors of various denominations. In the middle of my sermon, I posed the question "What would you do if you died today and went to heaven, and when you got there, you found people who had been Buddhists, Hindus, and even homosexuals walking around with Jesus? How would you feel?" Their response was unanimous: they said they would be *angry*. It's one thing when we have information that leads us to believe these people are going to hell because of their lack of knowledge of Christ. But it's quite another when we actually *want* them to go to hell.

The oft-repeated observation that "Christians shoot their wounded" didn't come about by accident. Though this is certainly not the truth for every Christian, it's accurate for many. This is a basic truth concerning the church today. We have no patience because we want people to suffer when they struggle with things we can't relate to. I don't believe we consciously feel this way, but deep within our subconscious, we do. It's how we believe our Father feels. We want people to pay for their shortcomings. After all, it's only fair. There's no such thing as a free ride. And many people feel they've been called to safeguard heaven from people who don't deserve to be there because of their actions.

God Is Patient

Perhaps the most exciting revelation I came to understand when I fell in love with people was that patience comes through understanding. Understanding comes through love. When you truly love someone, whether a spouse, a child, or a friend, you understand his or her heart. And when you understand someone's heart, you have patience.

Imagine if you worked in the emergency room of a hospital and one evening a two-year-old child was brought to you who'd had boiling water spilled down the front of his body. The child is screaming and wailing at the top of his lungs. As you delicately cut away his clothing, you see that his skin is melted away. My questions to you are these: What are the chances you would lose your patience with this child for screaming? Would you secretly wonder why his mother wasn't quieting him down? Would you even attempt to quiet this child? What are the chances that you'd even start to get irritated? You wouldn't, would you? You can see with your eyes the reason this child is screaming. You see the heart of what's going on and because of that, the symptoms don't stress you out. You don't even begin to lose patience because you understand.

Love is the same way. When you love someone, you will see the injured child in everything they do. Love's eyes look beyond the flesh and into the heart. People who lack patience are blind to the heart. Love sees into a person's heart because love both originates in the heart and is directed toward the heart. When looking for patience, we must turn to love to find it.

When my daughters were young, I often told my wife that our children were miracle workers because they could turn anything into whine. Because they were so close in age, they harmonized with one another while doing it. There were times when they cornered me and pinned me against the wall while whining on opposite sides. Sometimes, in the midst of this, *I forgot that I loved them* and started to lose my patience. It was always at the moment I took my eyes off my love for them that I lost understanding of why they were crying.

It's as though I became blind in an instant. Few things are more stressful than listening to screaming children when you have no idea what is wrong with them. As soon as I look at them and love them again, I suddenly see the problem. Perhaps it's because they are tired or hungry. Many times, it's because they feel insecure and they just need to be held. I have found it impossible to see the reason unless I am in tune with my love for them. My love for my daughters breaks through their outward actions and reveals the heart of what they do.

God is patient with you because He understands you completely. When He sees you struggling with sin, His eyes see past the sin and straight into your heart. He knows why you do what you do. His patience with you is not a case of holding back His boiling anger toward you, but that He knows you so well He doesn't even begin to get angry. Your Father sees the injured child in everything you do. His eyes see past the exterior and straight into the heart of who you are.

The greatest obstacle for most people to overcome is the fact that they think they know themselves. This is why we generally can't receive compliments from people. We honestly think we know better. What we know about ourselves is usually a set of facts about what we have done and where we have been. This is not what God focuses on when He looks at you. His focus is always on your heart. Within the heart lies the truth about who you really are. You just might be surprised at how pleased God is with your heart.

God is patient with the speed of your personal growth. There is never a time when He loses patience with you because you aren't getting something fast enough. God cares about the beginning and the end of your life. He is not the slightest bit irritated at you when you repeat the same mistake over and over. God understands, and He is patient because He's in it for the long haul.

My wife and I attended a baby shower recently where this truth beat me over the head for about four hours. I didn't want to be there. I would rather be a prisoner of war than attend a baby shower. From the moment we arrived, I began concocting a plan to leave early. My mind was racing a million miles an hour, looking for the cleanest escape. I had done everything short of faking a heart attack, when my wife finally looked at me and whispered in my ear, "Just decide in your mind that you are going to stay for the entire night, and your stress will go away." She was right. My impatience was brewing because I had not resolved to stick it out. The moment I changed my thinking, I was calm and relaxed, and believe it or not, I became a born-again metrosexual and had an embarrassingly good time.

This is what love does. God has decided wholeheartedly that He will be with you for all eternity. He has patience because He isn't even thinking of leaving or sneaking away. He is in it for the long haul, and because of that, He has a clear vision of the finish line. He knows the end of your story, and He is pleased with it. You don't need to worry about the timing of your death because your Father has it all under control. He is the author of happy endings.

Before my son was born, my wife and I took our four daughters to SeaWorld in San Diego. We had been planning this trip for a long time and had spent many hours preparing the girls for what Daddy had said would be "the greatest experience of their lives." As the weeks and days grew closer, they were eager with anticipation. Every night before bed, my wife and I would tell the story of how four little girls went to SeaWorld and met Shamu, the giant whale. We would show them pictures of dolphins flying through hoops and penguins playing underwater. We quizzed them on all the animal names like polar bear, sea lion, stingray, shark, and otter. They knew so much about SeaWorld that if it wasn't for their ages, they could have landed jobs there for the summer. At one point, we thought we might have to put the trip off another week because my youngest daughter seemed to be getting sick, but thankfully she recovered just in time. Finally, one day at four in the morning we entered their bedroom and gently picked them up and carried them to the car. We quietly strapped them in their car seats and started down the road to California. By the time they woke up, we were already halfway there.

Their suitcases were lovingly packed with clean clothes their mother had washed just days before their departure. The car was filled with their favorite toys and blankets, along with a healthy supply of snacks and juices. The glove box became a library of children's tapes and books. In the trunk we packed an ice chest, a video camera, extra diapers, two strollers, and just about everything else we could think of that we might need.

The day of our departure took a great deal of planning on our part. Though none of the girls knew when we would be going, their mother and I did. We had been preparing everything weeks in advance. All they needed to do was believe.

God's heart is like this about the day of your death. He's with you. He knows the time of your departure, and He is making sure everything will be packed and in order when that time comes. All you have to do is believe. God understands you better than anyone you will ever know. He is patiently preparing you for that day when you'll finally meet face-to-face. He is growing your faith, encouraging you, and continually bringing the things you need to make you into exactly who He planned you to be from the beginning. His immense love makes Him immensely patient. And because of that, we have no reason to fear.

CHAPTER 4

The Divine Manipulator?

As she walked through the door of my office, I was shocked. I could sense her intense pain from where I sat behind my desk. Through her delicate features, I could see a spirit that was surprisingly confused, worn down, and sinking fast. It was as if there were smoldering candles behind each eye that were on the verge of being snuffed out if something good did not happen soon. Behind an oversize handbag, her arms were folded in an effort to hide the obvious bruises and scratches that covered them. She appeared uneasy and nervous, like a child who was doing something wrong and was terrified of being caught. She began to stumble through some words, trying to find a place to start. I offered her a cup of coffee in an effort to cut through the tension in the room. Then, as if she had not even heard my words, she abruptly began her story. The opening was all too familiar, as I have heard it no less than a thousand times before.

"I met this guy."

What came next is what always comes next when a woman like this sits in my office: the usual long list of terribly unkind things "this guy" had said and done to her over the past six months. Then, as if she had not said anything she just did say, she casually, almost flippantly, allowed the words "but I know he loves me" to spill out of her mouth.

This young lady's perception of love represents one of the

biggest mistakes our generation makes about love. Countless women and men have given themselves over to this pathetic belief. What is so disturbing to me is the number of hurting people who simply believe that love does not need to be kind in order for it to be authentic. Many of us have grown so accustomed to unkindness that it doesn't even affect us anymore.

It reminds me of the "starving children" commercials on television. Precious human beings reduced to skin and bones with bloated tummies and peeling skin on their backs, crouched down in the streets, waiting to die. Their faces have that same dim look of death that this young woman had that day in my office. Their lips are swollen with open sores as flies buzz around their mouths. The image of the starving child with the flies on his lip has become somewhat notorious.

How dreadful must their lives be in order for them to *not* brush the flies away from their mouths? Could it be that in the midst of all the bad things in their lives, this pales so much in comparison that it's not even worth spending the energy to make it go away? The very thing that turns the stomachs of most Americans has become the acceptable norm for these starving children. And so it is with unkindness in relationships. It has become the "fly on the lips" of thousands of relationships. Perhaps it's because we are a generation that is starving for love. Though it's irritating to the soul, and it diminishes the spirit, it's not worth the energy to brush it away.

We have strayed so far from kindness that we have even forgotten what it looks like, and as a result we become easily deceived by its counterfeit. For every attribute of love, there is a counterfeit that looks like it, feels like it, and even smells like it, but it's actually the opposite. And so it is that kindness has been replaced with a horrible counterfeit that fools even the savviest person. It is my belief that people both inside the church and outside have bought the counterfeit of kindness without reservation.

The real problem with our swallowing this lie is that we ultimately perceive God's heart the same way. This becomes a terrible problem, one that closes the door to ever knowing the truth about our Father's heart.

The great counterfeit of kindness is *manipulation*.

When the antithesis of kindness, manipulation, is present, true kindness becomes voided out. In order for kindness to be authentic, it must have no ulterior motive behind it. The moment a hidden motive supports a kind act, the act itself ceases to be kind and suddenly becomes manipulation.

This is why most people's response to a kind act is, "What do you want from me?" We have grown accustomed to the lie. It is beyond our comprehension why anyone would do something nice without wanting something in return. We become skeptical and even angry if we can't immediately see a manipulative motivation behind someone's actions. It's intimidating when we first experience true kindness because it confuses us. It is suspended by love and nothing else.

I have seen it hundreds of times in my life. A man compliments a woman and speaks seemingly kind words to her, just before he asks her out on a date. All the nice things he said to her immediately blind her. Something deep in her heart makes her uneasy, but she pushes it back down and agrees to go out with him. Her heart knows that his "kind words" were followed by a come-on, but her flesh kicks in and convinces her head that he really meant those wonderful things he said. Finally, after giving a sizable chunk of her life away, she comes to her senses and breaks up with him, only to repeat the same scenario in a few months with someone else who tells her what she wants to hear.

The problem with being fed synthetic kindness is that over time people develop a taste for it. When they are faced with the real thing, they are repulsed by its flavor. This poses a staggering problem in our relationship with God. Until we come to an understanding and develop an appetite for the authentic truth about Him, we will inevitably redefine His personality to fit our spiritual palates.

We are a generation of Christians who have become addicted to "God-flavored kindness" that has nothing to do with the actual truth of who He is. That skewed picture of God can actually be something so ugly and repulsive that you would think any normal person would run like crazy to get away from Him, but amazingly people train their palates to actually crave this lie and ultimately prefer it over truth.

It's like men who have finally given themselves over to the belief that women like to be treated badly. Sadly, some women are indeed attracted to this. This is simply the evolution of what love has become. The bad boy gets the girl while nice guys finish last.

Strangely, this demented pattern holds true for many Christian people when it comes to their theology. The more abusive it is, the more attracted to it they become. I constantly marvel at how many people are repulsed by the grace message. To them, grace is the most unattractive guy in the room and they despise his very existence.

For many people, their relationship with their religion is eerily similar to an abusive relationship between husband and wife. Like the woman who visited me in my office, people are routinely battered, beaten, and abused, but rather than see it for what it is, they blame themselves. They say things like, "If I were a better Christian this wouldn't be happening," or "I deserve this because I have this or that in my life." Ultimately they find some twisted way of rationalizing that this abuse is good for them and needed for spiritual growth. Because their view of kindness has been turned upside down, they see it as evidence of love rather than proof of its absence.

The proof that American Christians believe this way about God is seen quite clearly. We have been taught to use kindness as a manipulative tool to get people to do what we want. We have mastered the art of "acts" of kindness. We get together and invade a neighborhood with acts of kindness such as cleaning graffiti and picking up trash, but our next-door neighbors have no idea we are Christians. This is so because kindness is not in our hearts. It's a show we've been taught to put on for the world for one reason alone: to get them to go to our church. It rarely has anything whatsoever to do with wanting to touch someone's heart. We are known for being insincere and having ulterior motives behind everything we do. We are this way because we believe our Father in heaven is this way.

Because of our belief in the counterfeit, we believe that the blessings of God directly parallel the amount we give in the offering plate. Everything about God's heart has been turned upside down in our spirits by this counterfeit. Christian theology has now changed the truth of authentic kindness, which says, "Freely you have received, freely give" (Matt. 10:8 NIV), and flipped it upside down to mean, "If you give, you will receive." This is perhaps the most horrendous deformity we have placed on the face of God in our generation. It is a direct reflection of the devil himself, and we attribute it to God without even second-guessing ourselves. What is even more disturbing is that most Christians actually like it that way because they can always calculate on paper exactly where they stand with God. The problem with this mentality is that it's not conducive to relationships. No one wants to be friends with a manipulator.

Most people believe in a manipulative God who has a self-seeking motive behind everything He does. This is why we don't trust Him when He does something nice for us. It takes us by surprise. If we have a bad habit or sense we're doing something wrong, we expect nothing from Him until we get our act together. If He does bless us, we immediately begin to wonder what we're supposed to do for Him in return. When someone we know who *isn't* living a holy life receives a blessing from God, it confuses us and makes us angry because he or she surely didn't earn it. Most of the time, however, we don't even see when God does something kind for us because we're too busy assessing whether or not we deserve it. Christians today are more apt to attribute hurtful things in their lives to God than they are kindnesses.

Kindness *always* lands in the heart. The counterfeit of kindness is directed to the flesh or the head. These things pass away, but things of the heart last forever. Kindness is an attribute of love, and love lasts forever, so kindness must be aimed at the *forever* part of you for it to be authentic. Many have lost sight of this mandatory aspect of kindness because they have lost sight of their hearts. Most people today don't even understand the difference between their hearts and their heads. This is why cheap imitations of kindness fool us so easily. We are fooled by things that make sense to our heads but have little or nothing to do with the truth of our hearts.

Because the counterfeit of kindness is purely temporary, many have learned to see God as a pursuer of temporary things. Today's real measure of His kindness is in how much He rewards the flesh. Financial blessing is the biggie. We even secretly judge people who are struggling financially because we think they must not be right with God. Kindness has nothing to gain in return and thus defies human logic. When someone experiences true kindness, they almost always look as if they've seen a ghost. Supernatural things scare us to death. They make us feel helpless and insecure because we have no control over them. The humbling feeling that real kindness elicits in our hearts is scary and overwhelming. This is why we feel we have to return the favor. But until we're able to receive authentic kindness, we will never know God's heart.

Anyone can do a nice thing. It doesn't require love, but a kind thing *always* hits the heart because it is directed by love. Niceness is appreciated; kindness brings you to your knees and exposes intimate parts of you that you've kept hidden all your life. This is why we would rather have people be nice to us than kind. Niceness keeps its distance, but kindness *invades*. Niceness makes us smile, but kindness can make us cry. Niceness pats us on the back, but kindness reaches into the heart and massages it. Niceness asks "How are you doing?" but kindness really wants to know the answer. And usually, it already does.

In counseling sessions, I am always amazed at how confused some people get when they find out what God really wants to say to them. It's as though they are expecting Him to confront their every sin. They walk in with a mental list of things they should or shouldn't be doing, and God hits them in an unexpected place. Just when you think He is going to call you on your lust problem, He tells you that you are loved and He is proud of you. The moment you think He's about to expose your gossip habit, He breaks in and whispers to your heart that you are indeed worthy of friendship and you should trust that about yourself. Right about the time you think God is going to chastise you for smoking cigarettes, He calmly tells you about the wonderful future He has planned for you.

God is this way because He knows that the cause of your personal struggles is found in your heart. He is not so shallow that He has to confront the symptoms of a burdened heart. He confronts the heart directly because that's who He is, and that is what He cares about. Everything about you originates in your heart, and your Father does not preoccupy Himself with the external manifestations of a broken heart. He keeps His eyes fixed on the prize at all times. Financial blessings and things that pertain to the flesh are nice, but God is kind. His kindness and His niceness are worlds apart. One man may receive ten thousand dollars the moment he needs it but not be touched in his heart, while another man receives a stuffed toy in the hospital and is moved to tears. God's promise to you is to provide the temporary things you need to survive, but His kindness cares about your heart.

God is an expert marksman. Because He loves your heart so much, He knows it even better than you do. He has memorized it and has written it upon His heart. He aims only for the most intimate part of you, and He hits the bull's-eye every time. Sadly, many of us miss Him and live powerless lives because our eyes are on our flesh and not our hearts.

Because of where kindness is aimed, it always produces stunning results. There is a power in kindness that topples strongholds and crushes addictions. It softens the minds of stubborn people and deflates the pride of the arrogant. Kindness is more powerful than anything the flesh manifests. Nothing can stand up to it. You will know when it's authentic, because the deepest parts of you will be moved and transformed by its presence.

We have been taught to believe that the fear of God's wrath is what brings us to repentance. Hell has been held over our heads by preachers who believe that fear is the greatest motivator to the human spirit. Fear has gained such respect over the years that most people would attribute more power to it than to kindness. The problem with this way of thinking is that fear pertains to the flesh, and everything of the flesh will soon pass away. It's temporary, but kindness is eternal. People do not respond to threats of brutality and abandonment for long. Threats may work for a time, but eventually they lose their power. People respond to the kindness of God, because we were created in His image. Because we are eternal beings, we respond best to eternal things.

Your Father in heaven is compelled in one direction every time He lays eyes on you. He is constantly drawn to that part of you He loves the most. Your heart! This is why we think He is so mysterious. We have lost sight of our hearts. Just when our flesh cries out for one thing, God answers with another. Generation after generation, we struggle to identify the motives of our God by how they pertain to our flesh and therefore end up confused and dismayed. Until we realize what He cares about, we will always find Him impossible to understand. When we finally grasp God's focus, He will suddenly become real and knowable.

My life changed when I began to understand that my *heart* is the desire of His heart. It's the center of His attention. He coddles it and cherishes it; He adores it and admires it. To Him, your heart is like a beautiful diamond that entrances a young woman. He is mesmerized by its many facets and hypnotized by its beauty. Your heart is a priceless jewel that the jeweler washes and puts under light to watch it gleam and sparkle from every imaginable angle. Everything within Him desires to gaze upon this part of you. His work in your life is honed in on this one place. When He speaks to you, He speaks to your heart. When He touches you, He touches your heart; and when He is touched by you, it is by your heart.

God is kind. He is always kind. His kindness drives Him

to move your heart with no strings attached. He shows kindness not to manipulate you to do things for Him, but because that is who He is. He is hopelessly driven to the most intimate part of you.

My friend Mike is a former Green Beret who served his final mission in Desert Storm. He was awarded a Silver Star in that war for heroic acts in the heat of battle. While on a mission, a missile shot down Mike's helicopter and he was the only survivor. Every one of Mike's buddies that he loved and cared for was killed in the crash.

By the time help arrived, they were amazed to find that in spite of a broken neck and back, a dislocated hip, shoulder, and ankle, and a bullet wound to his abdomen, Mike was miraculously unloading the bodies of his friends from the burning chopper. He was given a Purple Heart. They pinned it to the full body cast in which Mike spent the next six agonizing months lying motionless, clinging to life. In the midst of Mike's dealing with the haunting guilt and shame of being the only survivor of his platoon, the doctors informed him that he would never walk again.

Not only did Mike prove them wrong, but he later went on to carry the Olympic torch through the streets of his hometown in Nebraska. He became a local celebrity who was known for never giving up. Mike's inspiring optimism is outweighed only by his transparent childlike sincerity. It's the size of this man's heart that makes him my hero and a spiritual Green Beret in my mind.

Several years ago Mike called and invited me to lunch. He said he had something to give me. There was a seriousness in his voice that told me to brace myself, because something unusual was about to take place. He told me he had prayed about what to give me for Christmas, and after a week of contemplating it, he had decided upon the perfect gift.

After reaching into his car, he turned around and held out his hand. I almost fell on my face right there in the parking lot when I saw what he was holding. With an excited look of sincere generosity in his eyes, Mike presented me his Purple Heart.

This unbelievable gesture left me speechless. I just stood there flabbergasted. There was nothing I could say or do. I couldn't run to the nearest gift store in an effort to "even up the score," because money couldn't buy a gift that would even come close to this. Nothing short of handing over one of my children could compare to this. Mike was aiming for my heart, and he hit it. He hit the target in the only way it could be hit. He gave me his *heart.*

What a beautiful picture this is of God's heart. It is His desire to touch your heart in a way that will leave you speechless. The reason why God's kindness never has ulterior motives behind it is because His kindness simply cannot be repaid. All you can do is stand there and receive it. When God gave His only Son, He gave His heart! It was the only way He could *hit the target* of our hearts. His kindness is beyond the realm of *reimbursement*; it transports the human heart into a sphere where nothing but bare acceptance is possible. Only when the heart is touched can this be accomplished. Kindness is the only means of touching the heart, and God is the kindest of all.

Knowing the truth about Him changes everything.

CHAPTER 5

The Jealous God?

The day of the youth group Christmas party had finally arrived, and the house was overflowing with the sounds of laughter and music. I had determined to make this the best party these people had ever seen, and I would be the master of ceremonies. When it came to holding the attention of a crowd, no one could hold a candle to me. Within just a few moments, I was telling jokes, making funny faces, and in full control of the entire party. Everyone was laughing and egging me on, and I loved it. As people gathered around me, I became the star of the show for that wonderful moment. I had dreamed of this day and had even counted down the hours and minutes to its beginning.

About forty-five minutes into my captivating performance, an all-too-familiar sound began to drift from the family room. It was the haunting hum of my brother David playing the piano. Dave was several years older than me and had been taking piano lessons for most of his life. If that wasn't bad enough, he had also spent hours practicing and was quite good. So good, in fact, that he stole the show every time he played.

Before I could get to my next punch line, I found myself talking to an empty room. The entire bunch of my fickle friends had suddenly caravanned to the family room to gaze upon Maestro David as though they had never seen a boy play the piano before. They sat in silence with wide eyes and tapping feet as Dave played song after song. I truthfully thought it would never end. The moment he finished one song, some idiot would say, "Play another one," and so he did. On and on it went, like a broken record, until I thought I was going to scream. I found myself wanting him to hit a bad note or lose his place in the song just so they could see for themselves that Dave didn't deserve the attention he was getting. Of course, to my horror, he played beautifully. These people did everything but sing, "Play us a song; you're the piano man," for my brother that night. He played and played and played until the party was pretty much over.

As the guests were leaving that night, they were all talking about the "wonder boy" and his amazing musical talent, while my comical genius had been overlooked or forgotten. I can remember sitting in that room sick with jealousy. It was hard to breathe. I felt as though my bones were rotting inside. I wanted to take that piano and smash it to pieces.

The Heart of Envy

Medical science has proven that if it is done slowly and with the right antibiotics, the human body will actually accept animal organs. Scientists believe that one day it will be feasible to use the hearts of monkeys, sheep and even pigs to save lives. All it takes is the right drugs to persuade the body to accept the alien heart. The trick is in fooling the body into believing that this beastly organ is actually human.

This same concept is true when it comes to our corrosive perceptions of love. It is astounding to see what people will accept over time. We are routinely fooled by the counterfeit until many people's spirits and souls are functioning with a version of love that bears a resemblance to the heart of a baboon. It doesn't happen in a day, but gradually over time. And in the spiritual case, instead of saving a life, before we know it, the counterfeit makes our hearts think and believe things that are absolutely hideous and unacceptable.

When envy or jealousy is presented in its most raw form as it was in my story, it reeks with an obvious odor. Surely no one would mistake its ugly presence for being love. It stands in such opposition to what love is about. I have found, however, that over the years we have all experienced a gradual transition in our thinking. When it comes to love, not only have we learned to accept the opposite, but we actually expect it.

Envy is ugly and self-serving. At its core, it's jealousy. Envy and jealousy are *anti-relationship*. This attribute of envy leaves a person in constant "receive mode." The "give mode" required by love becomes shut off and even nonexistent, making relationship impossible. Selfishness leads to relational death, and jealousy is a frantic *self-protection* that paralyzes relationships. Born out of self-love, it leaves nothing for the other person. Nothing can survive it.

We say we don't believe that love envies, but when you think about it, many of us believe that envy is the true inception of love. We believe that without it, love can't even begin. Selfish envy can be equated with lust. Envy and lust share the same heart; they are fueled by a fleshly desire to gratify one's self. Our generation doesn't even believe that love is possible between a man and a woman without the initial presence of lust. If a friend wants to introduce you to a friend of the opposite sex, your first question is bound to be "What does he or she look like?" The treasure within is not nearly as important as the outside.

We've learned to present ourselves in a certain way to incite lust. Having someone lust after us is how many of us find our personal value. Our world has taught us that if we are sexually unattractive, we are worthless, and I believe that, sadly, most people in this generation have bought into that idea. Women especially have been taught to actually desire the look of lust from men when they enter a room. This look is envy in its most raw form. Many people have become addicted to the look of seduction, and they can't find their personal worth without it. Envy and lust share a common heart; they both *take* from others for personal gratification.

I've watched women in clothing stores purposefully buy things that will entice such looks from men. They don't even realize how obvious their intentions are to those around them. They put the jeans on and immediately turn around to see what their backside looks like. They put the blouse on and check their cleavage in the mirror. Many times they'll ask their girlfriend how their backside looks in the pants they're trying on. It's all an attempt to acquire that seductive and selfish response from others. How ironic.

The problem with inner treasures is that they can't be possessed by another person for personal gratification. They can only be admired. Selfish people have nothing personal to gain by discovering someone's inner beauty. The outer beauty is quite a different thing. That can be seen, touched, taken, and used. It requires no intimacy or emotional closeness. This is why so many people put the flesh at the top of their list of desires in a mate.

Because people believe that love *does* envy, they attribute it to God's character as well. When I fell in love with the people in my congregation for the first time, my eyes were opened to how widespread this upside-down view of God's heart has become in modern-day Christian thinking.

I have heard preachers thunder from the pulpit that "God is a jealous God." Because we see God's jealousy and envy from this upside-down human perspective, we have created a black cloud over Christianity that ultimately strangles to death our relationship with God. Envy, lust, and jealousy are synonymous. All three leave a person in constant receive mode, and their heart core is "anti-relationship." Jealousy is a frantic self-protection frenzy that completely paralyzes a person relationally. It is born out of self-love and absolute apathy for the other person. Nothing can survive this!

We are being conformed into God's image. If He does it, we can do it. If He doesn't do it, we are not supposed to do it. This is why it's imperative that we know the truth about His image. Whatever we believe to be true about Him is what we will ultimately be changed into. If we believe that God envies and is a jealous God, we will ultimately become envious and jealous people.

Unfortunately, our human perspective of a *jealous* God has attached itself to every slice of our religion. The results are catastrophic. We have become like the terrified woman who is enslaved to her husband's jealousy problem. She can't have friends or a life of her own because her world centers on her jealous husband. She rationalizes to herself that he acts this way because he loves her, but deep in her heart she is confronted with the truth that he doesn't even know her and his motives are based on love for himself. The most she can do is follow his rules and make him think he is the only one in the world that matters. Hopefully, if she proves herself to be faithful, he might release his death grip on her and give her the few remaining crumbs of her life back.

As awful as this sounds, it is astonishing how frequently I hear Christians talk about their God in this same repulsive manner. Because of our misconceptions about God, we have become just like this woman in our relationship with Him. What is worse is that, for the most part, we don't even know we are doing it. We've grown up with it all our lives, so it's not that upsetting. We begin to see through the same demented mind-set as the woman who translates jealousy as the result of love.

Think of this. We say things like "God wants you to give Him your life," and it doesn't even sound bad to us anymore. Over time it actually begins to sound beautiful. We even encourage others to give their lives to Christ because we are certain that this is what God wants.

Christ came that *you* may have life and have it more abundantly. He never asks you to give Him your life. *It's your heart He is after.* Only an envious God would give you life and then require you to give it back to him. He gave it to you, and He wants you to enjoy it to the fullest.

This upside-down thinking is seen when Christian musicians are plagued with the notion that their songs must all be about Jesus. If they dare to write a song about anything other than God, the Christian community scoffs at them. Their faith is called into question and they are ultimately viewed as backslidden. It is heartbreaking to God that this wonderful gift of expression is never allowed to express itself freely because the receiver of the gift believes that God would be jealous.

Many Christians are skeptical about listening to any secular music because they believe that God would rather have them listen to Christian music or nothing at all. This mentality is born out of a belief that God envies. They think He might get jealous if they gave any part of their day to something other than Him. They see Him as a jealous husband who doesn't want them to have lives of their own. They're encouraged by their Christian friends to go through their houses and throw everything away that doesn't glorify God or pertain to Him. How sad.

I've watched in amazement while people check themselves to make sure they don't love their mates too much, for fear that God will get envious and either remove their mates or remove His presence. I've seen dating couples even break up because the partners fear that the person they are in love with has become an idol before God. They constantly measure whether or not their thoughts are more focused on God than on the ones they love.

Several years ago, a young couple came to me for advice concerning their six-month-old baby. This child evidently had suffered from a string of recurring medical problems that seemed to be getting worse. I almost began to cry as I listened to them explain their theory as to why this was happening to their baby.

This poor couple blamed themselves, because they felt they might have made their child "an idol" in their lives. Because of the fact that they loved this baby so much and had given everything over to him, they believed that God was allowing illness to attack their baby out of jealousy. Poisoned by modern Christianity's interpretation of a jealous God, they even quoted a Scripture from the Bible that said God would destroy any idols that His people set up in their hearts before Him.

There is a look I give my wife that can be described in only one way. I cherish her. It's a deep, soul-piercing gaze that travels way beyond the surface and lands deep within her spirit. It's a look that sees every hidden thing within her heart and adores it all unconditionally. My eyes literally scream "valued" to her when she looks into them. When my wife sees that look in my eyes, she knows that I've discovered another beautiful thing about her. She finds her inner value because she sees me finding it every time I give her that cherishing look.

The same is true with my children. They see their value in their daddy's eyes. They find their self-worth in it. They discover who they are by seeing their reflection in their father's eyes. They know beyond a shadow of a doubt that I deeply cherish them. They know that there is a treasure within them because they see the reflection of it glowing in my eyes when I look at them this way. It's a look that says, "I would die for you," but also "I have already died for you. I'm not thinking of myself; only you." Only in this kind of death to self can such a look exist.

Inside every one of us is a treasure chest that waits to be opened by our Father. Until a person is cherished, his or her treasure chest remains closed. The cherishing look happens when the one giving the look has discovered inner value in the one they see. I've seen many people wait an entire life-time for just one person to discover value in them.

When that look comes from our Father, we know for certain who we are. Because we are a fatherless generation, most of us were never cherished by the one person we really needed it from. And we've become lost as a result.

God is a jealous God, but He is jealous on behalf of you. He is not selfishly jealous as human beings are. His righteous jealousy is actually the opposite of what we understand jealousy to be. Until we understand this principle of God's heart, we will always see Him upside down from what He really is. We have taken the Scriptures that describe Him as a jealous God and have given them a selfish and Satanlike interpretation. It has become so common that we don't even recognize it anymore.

When the Bible says that the Holy Spirit envies, it's speaking in the context of love. A father gets jealous when his daughter is dating a man who doesn't love her as much as he does. He's not jealous on his behalf. His jealousy is on behalf of his daughter. He wants her to have the best, and when he sees her giving herself to someone who doesn't see or understand her heart the way he does, he immediately becomes jealous for her.

God is not in competition for your love. I am always mystified when I hear people boastfully say, "I love God more than my wife." The only way to love God more than your spouse is to love God *through* your spouse. Your husband or wife would be the direct recipient of that love. Don't ever think that He will even raise such a question as to whom you love more. He is quite all right with you giving all of yourself over to your mate. The God who is love loves it when we love. He doesn't concern Himself with whether or not someone else is receiving more than Him.

I once approached a little boy in our church and told him what a good boy I thought he was. I was mortified when this five-year-old child began to inform me that he was a "bad little boy" and a "stupid little boy," and there was no good in him. As I walked away with a heavy heart I thought, *What kind of parents does this little boy have?* This is what the world thinks when we talk this way about ourselves in an effort to bring our Father glory. It's morbid and twisted. It paints a picture of our heavenly Father that is cold and ugly.

God is never in competition with your love for people! *Anytime you love a person, you are not far from God.* Your love for people is the evidence that *God is living inside you.* It is impossible to love God more than you do people. All people are the direct recipients of our love for God. It is impossible to have a relationship with God aside from relationships with people. He doesn't get jealous or envious of our love for His people; He delights in it because that is how He created life to work.

It shocks me to see so many people who honestly believe

that God desires a separate and secret relationship with them aside from their family members. Many men will lock themselves in their prayer closets while their wives are in another room watching the kids alone. I call this adultery. It comes from a mentality that God wants His personal time with them separate from their wives. I am not putting down a personal prayer time, but I am confronting a mind-set that is directly against God's heart. If I stayed two hours in my office praying while my wife needed me downstairs with our children, that would not be called prayer; that would be called *sin*.

When I see that my daughters love one another with all their hearts, I am overjoyed. Never do I wonder whether or not they love me more than they do one another. As far as I am concerned, if they love one another, they do love me. The quickest way to my heart is to love my children.

Only selfish people ask the question "Whom do you love more?" Don't ever think God behaves this way. The moment we buy into this way of thinking, we will have permanently shut ourselves out from knowing His heart. A true relationship with God is impossible unless we love people. He is never envious of our love for others; He created it! God is love. Why would He ever contradict who He is?

God is not insecure. His heart is that you love people more and more. Release yourself to love wholeheartedly because your Father in heaven made you for this purpose. Jesus told us that the way to love God is to love His people.

It was at the very moment I fell in love with the people in my congregation that I came to know the deepest parts of God's heart. I immediately began to find specific attributes of His character woven into the love I had for others. When I analyzed that love, it would speak to me and reveal what it would and would not do. It told me many things and answered many questions about my faith that had kept me bound and miserable for so long.

This love did not speak audibly. I just suddenly came alive in my spirit. As if it had been there matter-of-factly my entire life. Suddenly I knew why love does not envy: because the very scent of selfish envy is repulsive when we love.

And just as love does not envy, it does not boast.

CHAPTER 6

The Rock-Star God?

When I was eight years old, my mother had remarried and we were living in Phoenix, Arizona. My biological father was living in Houston, Texas, at the time. Every summer my older brother Kevin and I would take turns flying to Texas to spend a couple of weeks with our dad. This was a time that I looked forward to throughout the entire school year. As summer vacation began to approach, I found myself drifting off during class, daydreaming about my upcoming visit with my dad. By the time school was out and my turn to visit him rolled around, the anticipation and excitement were almost more than I could bear.

I can remember the day when my brother Kevin returned from Texas with a new haircut, new clothes, and a backpack full of interesting new toys. This meant that I had only a month to go until I got to see my dad. I was exhilarated!

As Kevin took me into his room and displayed each new toy and article of clothing that Dad had bought him, I began to notice something different about his personality. It was something that made me feel small and insignificant. To put it plainly, he was being cocky. His voice had a cocky tone as he chewed on a piece of cocky gum that Dad had bought him. Even his stupid haircut looked cocky. His entire demeanor reeked of cockiness.

Over the next few days, my ten-year-old brother proceeded

to boast about everything he and Dad had done together. He casually mentioned names of people I had never heard of. He talked about places I had never seen. He told of experiences that were completely foreign to me, and because I was on the outside looking in, I couldn't keep up with the conversation.

It was obvious that he enjoyed the fact I was on the outside. I could see it in his eyes. There was something in him that wanted me to know for sure that I would never have the same relationship with our father that he had. It would not be as fun or intense. It would never be as close or intimate. And in just a few short days, my entire perception of how it would be with Dad went from glorious and thrilling to hopeless and dreadful.

By the time I boarded the airplane for Texas a month later, I felt empty and worthless. What I had dreamed of for so many hours just didn't seem as exciting anymore. I didn't even have the energy to try to make it fun. I had been officially *demotivated* by the boasting of my young brother.

When I gave myself over to loving people, I despised boasting even more because I knew from experience what it did to those in its path. Several years ago, I was asked to be the keynote speaker for a relationship conference in Texas. Halfway through the conference a group of the "head pastors" decided to take me out to a nice restaurant for lunch. Through our brief conversations just before we ordered our meals, I could tell that these men had an extreme respect and reverence for me. Their actions and mannerisms showed me that there was a certain intimidation they felt in my presence.

It wasn't long before our food arrived, and I was asked to pray for the meal. I bowed my head and said, "God is great, and God is good, and we thank Him for this food. Amen." When I looked up, what I saw has made me chuckle for years. Many of them looked dismayed and confused. It was price-

less. It was a combination of total confusion and utter letdown. Several of them nervously laughed while the others sat
in judgmental dismay. Their view of my spirituality as being
superior to theirs was destroyed.

I didn't do it out of spite. I simply felt I had to burst their
bubble. I knew that if they had me on a pedestal, they would
ultimately feel like I did that day with my brother. I didn't
want them to feel a million miles away from their Father. I
couldn't stand the thought of them cowering away from God
because they felt they couldn't add up to what they thought I
had with Him. I didn't want something like an ultraspiritual
food blessing to cause them to feel inadequate or inferior in
their spirituality.

I have found only one undisputed way of lifting people
up. It may not be popular or spiritually attractive, but it
always works. The best way to lift hurting people up is to get
beneath them.

In my travels, people often thank me for "being real." I
think they mean they can identify with me. I didn't leave
them feeling like I had arrived at a perfect spiritual plane
they could never reach. They felt they were on my level and
if I could do it, so could they. I do this for one reason and one
reason only; I love them, and love does not boast.

When I fell in love with people I found that with everything in my heart, I wanted to meet them on their level for
their benefit. This is the opposite of boasting. Boasting is
bragging about our strengths, but if we truly love, we will
boast about our weaknesses for the purpose of elevating the
ones we love.

Boasting is bragging about the truth. It's exalting the highest
truth about a person, place, or thing. The problem with boasting is that it ultimately pushes others down around us. It leaves
people feeling like failures, or at the very least, inadequate. It

cultivates spiritual inferiority. Boasting is based on comparison thinking. When we boast, we are letting others know that they don't add up. When they don't add up, relationship is impossible. Love does not boast because love is only about relationship.

An unreachable person is not someone we human beings can relate to. We must be able to *relate* before we can have a *relationship*. People who claim to have reached a spiritual level that is far beyond the average person's ability to comprehend are usually pretty lonely people. They're lonely because there is no such spiritual level. I've found that people create this superspiritual facade as a subconscious way of retreating from intimacy with others.

This is the greatest obstacle I have to overcome when I go to a church to preach. Most people immediately believe several things about a guest speaker who comes to their church. They think that he is better than they are, or he has some special powers that they don't have. People will never give me their hearts until they know that I'm the same as them. The moment I get those stars out of their eyes is the moment I can connect with them on a truly intimate level.

I'll be honest with you. At first, I enjoyed the attention. It made me feel good. After all, there is a certain gratification that goes along with being famous. It feels good to have people think you're a spiritual guru of sorts. My flesh loved the entire exalted experience, but I had to give it all up because I truly wanted to help people, and I knew they would never connect with someone they couldn't relate to.

One of the main concerns I have after observing Christians over the last twenty years is that boasting has become a way of life. It has found its way into many churches and has become even more accepted in the larger world.

One of the biggest ways boasting is manifested is through what I call "God-told-me-ism." I'm talking about people who feel that they have to boldly and bluntly announce to the world that "God told them" to do this or that. It wouldn't be so bad if these people reserved their claims of divine revelation for things such as "God told me to go to college" or "God told me to write a book," but it seems with some people God dictates every jot and tittle of their lives. He tells them what clothes to wear in the morning, what roads to take to work, what to order for lunch, and what pen to use when writing a check.

The reason these people feel so inclined to inform the rest of us that they are hearing from God is not because they are, but because they want to ensure that *we believe* they are. They're trying to validate their spirituality in the eyes of the person they're talking to. The problem is that in doing so, they step on the hearts of everyone in the room. They leave people wondering why God doesn't love them or speak to them as much as He does that person. People walk away feeling there is something wrong with their Christian walk, and they ask themselves why they can't hear the voice of God with as much clarity as this person does. It causes people to give up because they feel a million miles behind. Ultimately, "God-told-me" people do more harm than good.

Sometimes, the spirit of boasting is played out in people's testimonies. Many times testimonies become a way to titillate the crowd. I have found that almost every time you investigate further into someone's rags-to-riches testimony, you find that it didn't happen nearly the way he or she told it. It is often exaggerated for effect. Christians have been taught to outdo one another when telling their stories, and in the process they exaggerate the truth to make their stories appear even more exciting. As a result, we create a God that doesn't exist. People are left wondering why God isn't moving in their lives the way He did in the lives of the people in all those amazing stories they grew up hearing.

Many people accentuate their testimony because they actually think they're doing God a favor. They're making Him "look good." I think most Christians are afraid that if people knew how things really happened in their lives, they might not be attracted to God. Boasting and embellishing the story, in an effort to make God a superman, is usually done in an honest effort to sell God to a lost world. We do this because we honestly believe God is a boaster and He likes it.

It also grieves my heart when I see people who have become "expert prayer warriors" (how's that for an oxymoron?). They know everything to say and just how to say it. It's amazing to listen to them confront the enemy, bind the demons, call down the blessing, and release the anointing. Their prayers sound like an ER doctor calling out orders in the spiritual realm in a language that only the truly educated can understand.

The most disturbing thing about all this is the look of spiritual insecurity on the faces of the poor people who are being "prayed for." When it's all over, they feel worse than they did before they requested prayer. They feel like loser Christians whose prayers are bland and boring. They feel a million miles behind the rest of the world in their spirituality. This boastful way of praying puts many precious people in such spiritual bondage that I sometimes wonder if they wouldn't be better off without prayer at all.

Boasting generally has the effect of making people smaller. It shrinks their self-esteem and diminishes their spiritual confidence. Boasting has an anti-relationship quality that paralyzes people's hearts and forces them into emotional and spiritual seclusion.

What would cause us to pray or speak in a way that is boastful? It seems so clear that love wouldn't boast, right? Could it be, perhaps, that we are doing what we believe our

Father in heaven does? I want you to go through what you've been taught about God and think about that for a moment. Does God boast? I truly think it would be impossible for any Christian in today's church world to think otherwise. Most of us think it's okay because, after all, He's God. He has a right to boast. We think He boasts about His accomplishments, and we think He boasts about how great He is. This is why we amplify these two things in our church services.

We have scientifically based teachings that walk us through the pain and suffering Jesus must have gone through during the Crucifixion. We make movies that dramatize the flogging and beating He underwent on our behalf. At Easter we put together pageants and invite outsiders to come and watch Jesus get the tar beat out of Him for their sins. We have come to believe that it is in God's heart to hold this moment over the heads of His children in an effort to get them to obey the rules. If we are graphically reminded of the pain and suffering He underwent on our behalf, perhaps we will do our best to repay Him by living a right life.

The God I grew up with was like the mother who constantly reminds her kids of the pain she went through during childbirth in an effort to guilt them into doing what she wants. By the time I was sixteen years old I had witnessed more than a thousand reenactments of the Crucifixion. Over a hundred preachers had reminded me that Jesus "took the nails for me" and "hung on a cross for me." Even our Communion services, rather than being a time of remembering Him, had been reduced to going through a list of the awful things He went through on our behalf. Sadly, the gospel message has been affected by this way of thinking. "God loves you; come to Him," has been turned into, "Jesus got a major beating that was meant for you, so come to Him."

Does God boast?

God Does Not Boast

In the Old Testament, there is the story of when Moses went up on the mountain to get the Ten Commandments from God and a great cloud covered the mountain. The people couldn't get anywhere near the mountain or they would be put to death. The book of Exodus tells of the earth trembling, and the thunder, smoke, and lightning that accompanied that incredible experience. Everyone trembled with fear for their lives and begged Moses to go alone to approach God on their behalf.

But how does God want *you* to relate to Him?

Elijah had an encounter with the prophets of Baal where he challenged them to call on their gods to burn up a sacrifice. Despite all the prophets' ranting and raving, nothing happened. Then Elijah stepped forward and called on God, and suddenly fire fell from heaven and consumed the sacrifice completely. This unquenchable fire even licked up the water in the trenches surrounding the sacrifice. The people were astonished at the power of God and fell to their faces in reverence and awe.

But how does God want *you* to relate to Him?

Ezekiel had a vision of heaven where the glory of God filled the temple, and there were creatures suspended in midair giving praise and honor to God continuously. The experience was so incredible that Ezekiel could barely stand in the midst of it all.

But how does God want *you* to relate to Him?

The seas roll back and leave a path of dry ground at His command, the mountains tremble at the sound of His name, and the hills melt like wax in His presence. The glory of the Lord fills the earth, and nothing is impossible or too difficult for Him. He owns the cattle on a thousand hills and everything in between. He flung the stars into place and positioned the planets to His liking. At His very presence everything in heaven and on earth falls to the ground and cries, "Holy, holy, holy." His knowledge and beauty transcend every imagination of man, and His enemies literally dissolve into nothingness at the sound of His voice. He is everywhere at once; He knows all there is to know; and nothing exists that was not made by His hands.

But how does God want *you* to relate to Him?

Let me ask you this: Can you relate to a great cloud? Can you have intimacy with heavenly fire? Can you get close to a God who makes you melt? How does God want you to relate to Him? *The same way you would relate to a dirty, homeless carpenter.* I watch in amazement as Christians compete with one another in their efforts to describe the glory and majesty of God. They can analyze His splendor and radiance in the most articulate ways. They constantly meditate on His greatness and sing of His magnificence. Our worship songs declare the highest truths of His being. We are overjoyed at the power He possesses and the scope of His reign. We have even taught ourselves to speak in King James Version when approaching Him because it feels more reverent and holy. We do this because we honestly believe this is what God wants from us. This is how He wants us to see Him, and so we feel like we're getting closer to the truth about who He is when we remind ourselves of His greatness and majesty.

The way we view God today kind of reminds me of how we view rock stars. He has thousands of groupies who claim to know and love Him, but in the end it's not Him they adore; it's His words, His power, and His amazing good looks. His groupies aren't interested in knowing His heart. They are dazzled by all that surrounds Him.

This is precisely why God became a man. He wanted

us to know *Him* for *Him.* Though God loves the angels in heaven, they are basically groupies. All they can see is His glory and majesty. They can't help but cry, "Holy, holy, holy." God's incredible splendor and beauty are so overpowering that anyone or anything that comes into contact with Him immediately falls to the ground in worship and awe.

There is an *inner part* of God that remains hidden and veiled behind the radiance of His shimmering glory. It's a part of Him that is tucked so deep within the blinding brilliance of His presence that unless all that is great and magnificent is stripped away, no one can ever know this inner part of God. In Christ, God became nothing so He could have real intimacy with you. Jesus is the center core of who God is in His heart. He desires true intimacy with you so much that He shed all His outward glory and splendor so that you could make a clear-minded choice of whether or not to have a relationship with Him. This is the only way God can know for sure that you truly love Him.

God became something a little lower than you in order to lift you up! He not only became a man, but He became a servant of men and then died a criminal's death on the cross. One of the last things we see Jesus doing just before His crucifixion was perhaps the most astonishing example of a non-boasting God in all of Scripture. He was on His hands and knees washing dirty feet. God does not boast about who or what He is. He isn't interested in bragging about His highest truths. *Jesus Christ is God not boasting!*

Peter understood fully who Jesus Christ was, and he tried to put a stop to all the demeaning foot-washing. He refused to accept God in this way. He was much like modern-day Christians who are insistent on seeing the highest truths of His nature and nothing else. The response that Jesus gave Peter is His response to many of us today: "You must be washed by the Carpenter! You must know Me in this way if you ever want to have a part of Me." Unless you can receive the simplest side of God, you will never have intimacy with Him. It's impossible.

Imagine if a man broke into my home and was planning on killing my wife and children, but I convinced him to take my life instead of theirs. If he let them escape and then proceeded to take me into a back room and film himself torturing me for hours until finally taking my life, do you think I would ever want my family to see that videotape? Absolutely not! I would want them to remember my life and my love for them. There is nothing inside me that would ever want them to view the pain I underwent to save their lives. That would break their hearts. This is how God feels when we reenact the Stations of the Cross in an effort to riddle people with guilt and condemnation. It doesn't motivate; it exasperates. This is not what love desires.

Why are so many people more excited about the Crucifixion than they are about the Resurrection? God never boasts about what He went through to reconcile you to Him. The account of the Crucifixion lasts only a few sentences in the Bible, but the result of the Resurrection is seen throughout the entire New Testament. God does not boast about the Cross; He downplays it, and He rejoices in the possibilities of relationship with you today because of the Resurrection.

Don't ever feel that you have to repay God for the suffering He went through for you. This was a gift to you! Anytime we attempt to repay someone for a gift they gave us, we are diminishing that gift. An attempt to repay someone for a gift is really a rejection of that gift. You'll never know how much it cost to see your sin upon the cross because God removed the price tag from the gift before He gave it to you. Just receive it and go on. It's free. Boasters always expect repayment, and they make sure everyone knows what their gifts cost them. God is not this way. He never boasts!

God also never wants you to compare your relationship with Him to someone else's relationship. There is no comparison. What He has with you is entirely unique. No other person in this world will ever have what He and you have together. Don't ever wish your relationship could be like someone else's. He doesn't wish that.

The more I began to look intently into the heart of love, the more I began to know the truth about God's heart. I began to find that what I had been taught in church all my life was untrue. As my journey continued I began to discover a God who was more like me than I had ever imagined. Our next step in this journey might be the scariest prospect of all.

CHAPTER 7

The Proud God?

The unwritten rules of masculine conduct teach that men are to show little to no emotion. Emotion equals weakness and weakness equals sissy. The action heroes we have all grown up with are stone-cold and self-reliant. They're lone rangers who don't need anyone or anything. Nothing can penetrate their hearts because they already have all they need. Though they may help people in dire circumstances, they themselves never need the favor returned.

I can remember watching Charles Bronson when I was young. He was the final word in manliness, the real thing. No one else even came close. In other movies the hero always got the girl and rode off into the sunset with her, but not Charles Bronson. He even ditched the girl in the end. He didn't need anyone. He was an impenetrable island unto himself.

Perhaps there is a little Charles Bronson in every man. It's an image with which every man is familiar. We carry it into our marriages, our relationships with our friends, and even into fatherhood. It's the mind-set that says, "I don't need to be touched in my heart; in fact, I won't allow anyone to even have a glimpse of my heart."

At the core of this mentality is pride. Pride closes the heart and doesn't allow entrance. This is not the same as a person who has shut down their heart because of pain or insecurity. Prideful people honestly believe they don't need to be touched on a heart level by anyone. And this attitude produces some deeply destructive mind-sets.

Ask if love is proud, and most people will say no. Ironically, one of the most common complaints I hear in regard to relationships is that one or both people involved refuse to open up to the other. Over the years this little problem has worsened, and in today's society, it has reached a whole new low. Now a person is considered strong and "together" if they close themselves off from others. As a result, many people *do* believe that love is proud. We consider such personal pride a good thing and ultimately attribute such a personality to God Himself.

The God I was raised to believe in was a lot like Charles Bronson's character. He wasn't quite as heartless, but He certainly didn't need anyone. He was an island unto Himself. It was either God's way or the highway. I remember the preacher reminding us that God didn't need us, we needed Him, and if we ever confused that fact, God would make sure to straighten it out for us. It was okay for God to be prideful because He was perfect. After all, it's not considered prideful when it's true. God has no needs, and we were put here for one reason alone: to serve Him. The moment we step out of line or refuse to serve Him, He will cancel our passport to life without a thought. We are lucky to receive from Him, but to even think that He could need or possibly benefit from anything we could give is downright foolish. He has all He needs within Himself, and there is no possible way that we could benefit God other than to just do what He says.

Once again, many of us now define godliness according to this upside-down understanding of God. Pastors present themselves as self-reliant because they honestly think that is who God is. They believe that the closer they get to God, the fewer needs they will have. We've come to believe that the end result of being conformed to the image of God is that we won't need people anymore, because our fulfillment will be found within ourselves.

The things we teach about worshiping God prove that we believe God is full of pride. Many people say that worship is the reason we were put here; God created us so we could remind Him how great He is all the time. In pride, we tell ourselves that we worship out of obedience, because that is what God requires. We pat ourselves on the back, because at the end of our prayers we're careful to give Him and only Him all the glory. We spur one another on to serve Him like mindless slaves. And we believe that unless we do this willingly, He'll bring us to a "breaking point" where we fully submit to Him.

The picture we paint of God is not only prideful, it's disgusting. If we were to take the prideful things we say about God and attribute them to a person we worked with or someone we lived next door to, we would hate that person with a passion. We would avoid him or her at all costs. It would take nothing less than pure, stubborn dedication to continue a relationship with that person. But this is exactly the predicament with God we are in today. This is why we have to encourage one another to make a "commitment" to God. We even have "accountability partners" to keep us in line because if we were left alone, we'd slip back into avoiding Him completely. "Backsliding" is blamed for our natural response to the awful stench of a proud God. Nobody likes a prideful person. And nobody likes a prideful God.

As I said, this mind-set carries over into people's lives. I hear of husbands quoting Bible verses to their wives about how their bodies are not their own, trying to guilt them into having more frequent sex. How many women have come to see sex as a duty and not an expression of love? We believe

God loves for us to lift our hands and engage with worship music even when we're not feeling it or we're exhausted or suffering from sickness. We think God is as heartless and self-serving as a narcissistic husband who uses "the rules" to force his wife into sex. Such tangled teachings can only be the result of evil. Pride is not in God's heart. He doesn't need our worship. It's not even for Him. He wants relationship and worship that are mutually edifying, born out of oneness.

God Is Not Proud

So if it wasn't for worship, why did God create us? Did He have nothing better to do? Are we just a sea-monkey experiment He set up to watch from above? Was He bored? What was He thinking? Why would God, who has everything, waste His time creating a bunch of measly people? What could we possibly offer that He didn't already have a million times over? Surely God would be better off without the hassle.

The answer is perhaps the most astounding fact about God's heart I've ever found. And I found it only once I began to sincerely love others. It surprised me at first, and it will certainly surprise some people to hear it. It could dash a preconceived notion or two, or even redefine our idea of godliness.

Why did God create us? Because love requires expression.

Sure, He had a relationship with the angels. And who knows what other creations? But God also desired to express Himself in another way. And in some mysterious way, His love could not be completely love without us. We were, at least in part, a fulfillment of His longing. Does this imply that He didn't have everything He needed in and of Himself? Was He unfulfilled? No. But He put Himself on the line and became vulnerable in order to have a relationship with us and express His love. Why should this surprise us? We were created in His image. We have the same "need." We have a need for relationship, a need to be known and a desire to share ourselves with others. Consider a recent example from my own life.

After carrying our sleeping children to bed and giving the kitchen a quick once-over, my wife and I finally had some time to ourselves. Like so many nights before, we had rented a movie and were looking forward to snuggling on the couch and enjoying an evening of mindless entertainment.

Unfortunately, it was Angie's night to choose the movie, so I was sentenced to a sappy "chick flick." The movie she chose, however, did not appear to possess all the usual qualities I had come to expect from my wife's normal movie picks. It wasn't a love story or a romantic comedy. It was a true story about a man who had a fatal disease and was fighting for his life.

From beginning to end, this story was a tearjerker. It took all I had to keep from breaking down and sobbing. I found myself thinking about baseball, or work, in an effort to keep my composure. It wouldn't have been that big of a deal if it were not for my wife constantly leaning over to check to see if I was crying in the middle of the most dramatic scenes. For some annoying reason, Angie was determined to see me cry, and it was becoming irritating.

Suddenly, I was faced with an even more difficult predicament. Though I could easily keep my eyes dry by forcing my mind to wander, my nose was beginning to run. That wouldn't seem to be such a big deal, but sniffling could give me away. What would I do? After brainstorming to find a quick and easy answer, I nonchalantly mentioned that I had been fighting a cold. This allowed me the freedom to sniffle, and so I did. Unfortunately, she didn't buy it. The moment Angie heard me sniff she immediately leaned over and arrested me.

What she said next was what every man dreads. And what's worse is that she said it in a drawn-out "baby talk" voice.

"Hooonnneeey, are you cryyyyiiiiinnnng?"

"No," I replied, sounding totally offended. I couldn't say much more than that because the quivering in my voice would give me away. I immediately broke into a coughing spell hoping to redirect her to my cold. She didn't go for it and was now more determined than ever to catch me red-handed—or red-eyed.

It was no use. She had caught me. But in that split second as I was searching for a way to preserve my dignity, something extraordinary happened. It was so awesome I shudder to think I nearly missed it. My wife wasn't ashamed or let down by what she saw in me. In fact, something quite unexpected came over her. She was filled with something I hadn't seen since the day she first told me she loved me. Her eyes were twinkling with delight. It was as though she had finally found what she was looking for the entire time we'd been married.

That night, I watched as my wife fell head over heels in love with me all over again. All I could do was sit there and receive it. It was as if she needed to see me cry. It did something for her that words could not express. No amount of money, gifts, cards, flowers, or poems could reach this far into her heart. It took vulnerability on my part to get there. And I had arrived completely by accident.

God is looking for the same thing in you that my wife was looking for in me that night on the couch. Angie was bringing me to a breaking point because it moved her heart. There are places deep inside her that cannot be touched except by my vulnerability. She needs it. She needs to know that I am not impenetrable. It moves her in ways she cannot express. God is the same way with you, and the beautiful thing is that

God would *never* bring you to a breaking point unless He had already broken Himself. Being naked and spread-eagle on a cross is not about suffering as much as it is about total and complete vulnerability before the ones you love.

In creating us, God showed that He Himself was willing to be exposed as a sensitive, vulnerable being with the need to connect and experience authentic closeness. And He desired it with us, knowing we would struggle to see His heart and love Him in return. But He literally stripped Himself of all glory to expose the most vulnerable parts of Himself to humanity. And all because this was simply what was required to achieve an authentic relationship.

Though Jesus was a king, He had no problem becoming a carpenter. Though all glory belonged to Him, He was comfortable having no place to lay His head. Though His hands formed the entire universe, He actually enjoyed washing dirty feet. He enjoyed it, because these were the feet of people He loved. He did not require that anyone bow down to Him and give Him the respect He deserved. On the contrary, He invited them to walk with Him and call Him brother. Jesus wants you to know Him in the same way. There isn't a prideful bone in His body. It's not your fear and shuddering religious reverence He is after. It's your heart!

To say "God created us to worship Him" is as disgusting as me telling my wife that I married her for the sex. The fringe benefits were the furthest things from my mind. God is not that way with you. God created you because He wanted a relationship. With you. He wanted you to experience that. He desired a real two-way relationship that would be mutually edifying. When you have that with Him and you worship, you are ministering to His heart. You are touching Him, affecting Him, fulfilling His hopes out of what you share together. He is truly moved by you!

When I visit different places people compliment me because they want to edify me and feed my spirit. I appreciate it with all my heart, but when I return home and my wife tells me the same things, I'm penetrated clear to my soul. It hits me harder and empowers me because *she knows me.* There's a huge difference between someone telling me things out of distant respect and someone telling me they love what they *know* about me.

This is how God wants to be worshiped. His first and foremost desire is to be known by you. Worship is the consummation of that relationship. It can't precede relationship and be truly meaningful—not to mention beneficial to you. God is not a fornicator; He desires marriage first. Premarital worship is not how God operates. When you know Him, you worship what you know, and He doesn't sit there and receive it without returning the love back to you. His knowledge of you causes Him to explode with the same feelings you're expressing to Him. Remember, worship is not just for God. It's a time when *both of you* can express your love for each other. God is just like you in this respect. He loves it.

Just after our new baby, Jude, was born, many mornings after his bath I would hold him against my chest. There's something about your baby's skin that you can't get enough of as a parent. For that moment, I don't want anything between us. It's my way of getting as close as humanly possible to the one I love so much. It's all of him next to all of me. I love it!

When people are vulnerable and showing their complete selves, their needs are exposed. God has no lack, and His love is not need-oriented. He is complete and completely selfless. There is certainly some mystery here that's beyond our ability to understand, but this is usually why I'm so surprised to find people who view God's desire for their vulnerability as punishment or payback. If they only knew that God's stripping of His children has nothing to do with that—He does it because it warms His heart to see us that way. He wants all of us with all of Him, and nothing in between.

We think it's a sign of spiritual maturity to ask Him for little. We believe that the closer we get to godliness, the fewer needs we will have. Yet nothing could be further from the truth. There's nothing more heartwarming to a father than to express his love when asked for something he longs to provide for his children. And it's especially touching when it's something only he can provide.

This is God's heart for you! He's not offended when you ask Him for things. In fact, He's moved by it. He loves it. Especially when you believe that He can and will do it. It compels Him in a way that only a father could understand. He not only loves it when you ask, but He waits with expectation for you to ask because your asking fulfills His desire to provide for the one He loves. Anytime you admit your helplessness, God is inspired the same way I am with my children. Your vulnerability shakes Him at the deepest, most inner part of His heart.

Jesus told the people that He came not for those who didn't need Him, but for those who did. The thing that compelled Him to come was needs. Helplessness was the fuel that drove Jesus to do what He did. Helplessness inspired His miracles and healings. It was the central focus of His ministry.

Finding out that God was not proud has drawn me closer and closer to Him just as my wife was drawn to me. But when I discovered the truth in our next chapter, I found myself not only having the freedom to get close to Him, but I actually desired intimacy with Him for the first time in my life.

CHAPTER 8

The Offensive God?

While driving home from work, I was station surfing on my radio looking for something to help pass the time. After listening to several boring eighties songs that the disc jockey depressingly referred to as "oldies," I came upon a popular talk show host about whom I have heard many controversial things. I stopped briefly to listen, mainly out of sheer curiosity as to why he was so well liked. About sixty seconds into the show, I was appalled at his deliberate and calculated rudeness. Though he did have a sense of humor, it was apparent that his wit alone was not the reason for his massive following. The people who were calling in were genuinely entertained by this man's abrasive personality. What was even more astonishing was that everyone on the show seemed to have a real respect for this person's opinion. They actually praised him for being so "in your face" and for "telling it like it is." He was lifted up as a picture of strength and boldness.

I suspect that he rose to his level of fame because he spoke the things that were already on everyone else's minds. He even delivered his opinion with a tone and disposition that most of us secretly share, but refuse to express. It wasn't as though this man was abusive; he was just abrasive. He was rude. His career was timed perfectly because we live in a rude society.

You would think that things like rudeness would always be unattractive, but it seems this characteristic has taken an evolutionary turn in the last thirty years. Rudeness has become an accepted attitude. It's considered a selling point for talk show hosts and people in leadership. Rude men seem to attract women from all walks of life. Politeness and good manners have become a thing of the past. Thirty years ago, a man with polite qualities was considered a good catch. Today, however, he would be perceived as weak and frail. I am amazed at the number of women who think rudeness in a man demonstrates strength and confidence.

In the same way, many Christians believe God is rude and wouldn't have it any other way. They believe this is evidence of His strength and power. They cheer when it seems God has put someone in their place by publicly humiliating them or raining disaster on their livelihood. They'll exchange stories of how God got His point across to someone by exposing their hidden sin to the world. When we read Scriptures of Jesus' response to the Pharisees, we unwittingly insert a rude tone into His voice. We imagine Him talking this same way to people we don't like.

Over the years, I have watched a growing trend that has brought much concern to my heart. It seems to replay itself in almost every Christian circle at one time or another. It usually happens when a preacher is relating a conversation he supposedly had with God, and when he comes to what "God said," he presents Him with a callous tone that makes Him sound disrespectful and unloving.

I once heard an evangelist recall a conversation in which, he said, God was confronting him on a matter of personal pride. God supposedly said to him, "You make Me sick." Another time a story was told in which God's response to a person was, "Do I stutter or are your ears flapping?" These sorts of things may be done for humorous effect, but what does this do to the hearts of His children over time? Maybe people begin to expect that this is who He is and how He relates to us.

Have you ever had someone recall a conversation that the two of you had, and when they came to what you said, they used an abrasive and rude tone that was light-years from how you actually spoke? They misrepresented your character and disposition. Perhaps they even accused you of yelling at them, when that wasn't what happened at all. For some reason, they perceived you as a rude person, so when recounting what you said to them, they inserted rudeness into your words and actions. Do you remember how violated and misunderstood you felt? You were branded with a temperament that had nothing to do with the real you. This is how God feels when we do this to Him. It breaks His heart because these little stories ultimately turn the hearts of His children away from Him.

The problem is that we hear whatever tone we expect to hear. If we perceive God's personality as rude, we will hear only rude tones when He speaks to us. We'll underline passages in our Bibles that seem to fit our theory of His attitude. In fact, I have found most Christians almost never hear God because their ears are tuned in to a rude station. They are expecting either a correction, a rebuke, or a cold, callous direct order; and because this is all they've been taught to listen for, they rarely if ever hear from God.

Among all the definitions of rudeness I've found, there seems to be one common denominator: rude means *unfinished*. Not completed. A piece of wood that's unfinished, in a raw state, is rough and full of splinters. When that piece of wood is rubbed against someone, it causes one to bleed. Rocks that have not been polished are "rude." This is where we get the saying "rough around the edges." It speaks of the discomfort one might feel when encountering something or someone who's rude.

In biblical times, kings would use messengers to deliver their messages. These messengers were selected for their ability not only to deliver the words of the king, but to deliver the tone in which the words were spoken.

If the king threatened to go to war against an enemy, he would send his messenger to reenact the anger and rage the king displayed. If the king was screaming and pounding his fists on the table while he gave the message, the messenger would scream and pound his fists in the same tone and manner.

If the king invited people to a banquet and his spirits where high and happy, the messenger would act out that joy while delivering the invitation. This way, those who received it would hear not only the words of the message, but the disposition and tone as well.

Today, many of our messengers don't seem to reenact God's tone very well. It seems that the words of the Bible are all they need. The only way the Bible can be properly interpreted is if the messenger knows and understands the tone of the Author's heart. When a tone of condemnation and anger is given to words of encouragement and love, those words take on a different meaning that lacerates the heart and causes it to cower from God. It often takes years for God's children to recover from these fearful impressions.

This is why the Bible says to speak the truth in love. Truth ceases to be truth if it is spoken in any tone other than love. We Christians mistakenly believe that being truthful is the same as being "correct." One plus one equals two. But that is not truth. Truth is a person with a personality and that personality is love. Truth and love are interwoven together. If you take out love, you also take out truth. Have you ever spoken terrible things to a dog in a loving voice? The dog wags his tail and licks your face and excitedly spins in circles. Have you ever spoken words of love to a dog in an angry voice? The dog cowers and runs away.

This is why so many Christians are hiding today. Loving words have been spoken to them in an angry and unloving voice. Though they have memorized the words in their heads, they have also memorized the tone in their hearts. A preacher can tell his congregation that God loves them every Sunday for a year, but if that preacher doesn't love them himself, the tone of that message will be contaminated. It's not enough to preach on a subject and cover all the points. It must be alive in the heart of the messenger before it can be properly delivered. The message of love cannot be delivered with words alone. And because many preachers have attempted to do just that, we've learned to survive on being "correct" while never knowing the truth.

The teaching today in American churches to "respect the man of God" also demonstrates a rude or unfinished mentality. It's used to get people to do what the religious leader wants. Unfortunately, the work of Christ is denied by implying that there are some Christians who are men of God and others who aren't. In fact, the "men of God" in the Old Testament would have given anything to possess what you and I have today. They were called *servants* of God, whereas the New Testament says we are *sons and daughters* of God. All men and women deserve our respect equally.

I also see rudeness in how we claim that God orders us around as though He were talking to a child. We parents understand what it's like to have our kids incessantly question us. With our first child, I was determined to explain all her "whys." But five seconds into my explanation of why Daddy didn't want her to run into the street, she would interrupt me to ask, "But why?" I eventually retreated to the stock answer of, "Because I said so," which later gave birth to another stock answer: "You don't need to know why; just do as I say."

This may go over with our children, but the moment we try to use this line of reasoning with another adult, it becomes noticeably rude. It is rude because it disrespectfully assumes that incomplete and partial information is all a person deserves to get. It's a slap to their dignity; it challenges their competence. This is why I'm amazed when I hear people describe God as though He treats us with little or no respect at all.

We have built our theology on a rude God who says, "Do it because I said so." It's a safeguard against anyone who dares to ask why. We do this with the Bible more than anything else. Once the verse has been read, if you dare to ask why, your entire faith is on trial. The verse should be all you need. In other words, *"You don't need to know why; just do as it says."* No explanation required. Don't question it, or you will be labeled a rebel.

Truthfully, I believe that quoting Scripture is the escape route for thousands of pastors, evangelists, and authors today. It's something we have all learned to hide behind. It's easier than taking the time to explain our words to the listener because we know that Christians have been programmed to robotically agree the moment they see a scriptural reference. Christianity has injected a "because the Bible says so" clause into the hearts of modern-day Christians in an effort to cause them to give up individual thinking and blindly accept anything without question. To even ask "why" regarding the verse is misinterpreted as doubt. We believe this way because the God we have been raised with is flat-out rude. We've been taught to believe that He never negotiates or explains. The only thing He wants from us is obedience.

Many people now believe that blind obedience is a sign of spiritual maturity. We have come to see God as a rude slave master who isn't interested in our opinion; He just wants us to do what He says, when He says it. I have even heard people describe a true Christian as a broken horse who does only what he or she is told. No relationship is required beyond turning right or left when the reins are tugged. When we grow up hearing these ludicrous illustrations, it's no wonder we retreat from intimacy with God. Who would want a relationship with that?

God Is Not Rude

Though God is your Father in heaven, it's important for you to understand that He respects you. He doesn't treat you like a child. He understands that you are an adult, and He gives you the respect that an adult deserves. It concerns me when I hear Christians paint the "father-baby" picture. When we talk as though God is "spanking" us or He has put us in "time-out," we do not understand the truth about Him. These may be appropriate punishments for young children; however, when our children become adults, we show them honor and respect. God will never talk down to you or treat you as anything less than an adult. God respects your opinions and decisions. Believe it or not, He is even open to your input in certain circumstances. Not everything has to be done His way. An adult who is new to the faith is an adult nonetheless. I think the term "baby Christian" is extremely dangerous and degrading in this respect. Though it is popular to act as if God treats us like immature children, it's simply not true. He doesn't show respect for some and disrespect for others.

When my wife and I take our kids to the mall, we have

the same discussion when we park. Just before we open the car door, we sternly remind them that they aren't allowed to run in the parking lot. I caution them to obey their daddy and do what he says.

If someone were to ask my daughters to describe their daddy's heart, I would be truly grieved if they were to say, "He wants obedience." I desire their obedience for the sole purpose of their safety, but to define me as only wanting their obedience for obedience's sake hardly illustrates my heart. This is true as well with God's heart for you and me.

God never intended our relationship with Him to be like a soldier mindlessly following the orders of his commander. If you ask "why," He will help you understand. If you need time to get it, He will patiently teach you until you do. A relationship is a dialogue not a monologue. Our present-day view of obedience terminates the possibility of a two-way conversation.

God is truly an artist when it comes to you. Just like all artists, He sees the final picture long before He brings it into being. If you were to ask a great artist like Van Gogh what he saw when he looked at a blank piece of canvas, he might tell you that he saw swirling stars in the night overlooking a church nestled in the midst of rocky mountains. He would describe the brilliance of each color in the picture, and the mood it would give those who beheld it. A true artist sees the finished masterpiece.

Because of this amazing vision, and because it's a vision that most people do not have, artists will almost always cover their project with a white veil or cloth to hide it from the world until it is finished. As far as the artist is concerned, it is finished already, because it lives inside his heart. He covers it because he is protecting what is in his heart until it has been fully expressed.

Your Father in heaven is creating a masterpiece in you. The masterpiece that is you already exists deep within His heart. Make no mistake about it; He will never expose the things in you that are unfinished! I am startled to have met so many people who are truly afraid that God will expose them to the world. God does *not* expose your sin. He covers it.

The only exposing God ever does in your life is when He unveils the beautiful things about you to others. Just as my wife and I prod our children to recite the alphabet in front of dinner guests, He wants others to love you and be as proud of you as He is. The moment the guests leave, your Father returns to you with a paintbrush in hand and a twinkle in His eye and continues creating the masterpiece in you that He saw from the beginning of time. All that is rude and unfinished is covered with a veil of perfection.

One evening shortly after our church service had ended, the lobby was packed with people laughing and talking. My daughters had just been released from their class and were full of energy and excited to see their daddy. They were running in and out of all the people, searching for me, when one of my daughters lost control of her bladder and wet herself right there in the middle of the lobby. She did not know that I was close by and had seen what had happened. Her face immediately turned red, and she had a look of horror and embarrassment in her countenance that has etched itself into my soul to this day. As she looked around nervously, our eyes met, and she whimpered quietly, "Daddy, I went pee-pee."

Without even a pause, I scooped her up in my arms and covered her from the crowd. I held her close to my body and quickly found a nearby exit. As we nonchalantly headed to the car, I could feel my suit and tie beginning to soak. Not once was I tempted to hold her out away from me, but I squeezed her tight and spoke gentle, loving words in her ear and reassured her that no one saw what happened.

I was covering a masterpiece that was still growing. This is what fathers who love do. This is how God is with you. He will never expose your sin to the world. It deeply saddens me to hear so many Christians say the exact opposite about Him. From the beginning of time, God has been in the business of covering up sin. He soaks it up into Himself and away from you. Do not fear that God will ever humiliate you in order to humble you or teach you a lesson. Exposing an unfinished person is rude. He is great at keeping things just between you and Him. You are His masterpiece, and He will protect you and cover you until you are complete.

One of the statements I hear the most from people when I inquire about their relationship with God is this: "God has me in a wilderness." It's as though God has left them on top of the refrigerator like an avocado waiting to ripen. Many people actually believe this is who God is. They see themselves as being in a perpetual state of incompletion, and they honestly believe that God not only endorses this idea but He also participates in it.

This mentality goes against the basic theology of Scripture. In New Testament times, if you were a Christian you were in the Promised Land, not the wilderness. The wilderness time was before you were saved. Make no mistake about it; God will not put you in the wilderness! It was His intention to bring the Israelites through the wilderness. They are the ones who chose to stay because of fear. Later the Israelites received the entire Promised Land in one day, but they possessed it bit by bit. Just because you may have trouble accepting and possessing what God has freely given you, don't think He has put you in the wilderness. The only wilderness in your life is the wilderness you choose to live in, but you must know that God did not put you there.

God brings all things to completion, and He leaves nothing unfinished. Though you are a work in progress, He has already declared you completed! By one sacrifice He has made you perfect forever. When He looks upon you, He sees only the finished product. What were Jesus' last words? He said, "It is finished." He doesn't treat you as anything less.

I am sometimes baffled to find that many Christians actually want a rude God. They'll search the Scriptures to find the perfect scenario where God would for sure leave them for making a mistake. They debate heatedly with anyone who would suggest that they had any kind of security with Him, though Jesus said, "I will never leave you nor forsake you." Entire theologies are built on a rude God who hasn't resolved in His mind to stay with us forever. This constant state of *insecurity is the power of religion*, and anyone who subscribes to a theology they can't trust will inevitably be forced into a vicious circle of bondage, fear, and constant spiritual unrest.

Something happens in the mind and behavior of a marriage partner when he decides once and for all that he will never leave. He doesn't interact the same way with his spouse from that point on. He weighs his words and tone carefully before he speaks because he knows he'll have to live with whatever mess he creates with his partner. When you have a "*forever*" mind-set, you take great care of your relationship.

God is never rude to you for one basic reason: He has resolved to be with you forever in a marriage relationship. Divorce is never in His mind when it comes to you. He will never leave you, and because of this fact, He treats you in the same way He desires to be treated by you. That's right. The author of the "Golden Rule" not only wrote it for you, He follows it Himself. It was created *for* relationship by the One who desires a relationship with you.

As our walk through the heart of love continues, we are finding that our old perceptions of God's heart must be released and demolished altogether. And that's no truer than in the next chapter, one I believe is the most important of all.

CHAPTER 9

The Needy God?

My parents had been acting strangely for a number of months, and there seemed to be an unusual tension in the air when they were together. One night, I could hear my mother crying when she thought my brother and I were asleep. I remember hearing whispered arguments between stretches of my mother sobbing. From my room, I could make out only pieces of their conversation, but my mother was pleading with my father to consider how "this would affect the kids." He was quiet. If I hadn't seen his car lights through my bedroom window an hour earlier, I might not have believed he was even there. I waited for a response, but nothing came. The sound of my mother crying made me feel strange in my heart, like I was doing something wrong by hearing it. I knew this wasn't meant for my ears. So I never mentioned it.

Several weeks later, my parents called us into their bedroom. First my brother Kevin went in and they shut the door behind him. I sat on the living room couch with my eyes fixed on the bedroom door down the hall. What could be happening? My six-and-a-half-year-old brain was trying to piece everything together as quickly as it could. It was like waiting to go into the principal's office. My heart was pounding and my palms were wet. Finally the door opened and out came my brother. He had a cold, stoic look on his face, like someone had brainwashed him. He disappeared into another room. My mother's face was red and her eyes were swollen. She had a tissue in her hand, and her hair looked as if it had not been washed in a few days. Then she motioned for me to come to her.

The walk from the couch to the bedroom has stayed with me for almost thirty-five years. I remember every step. The air got heavy as I approached the room where they were. It was an overcast day, and the light through the windows was dim. When I came to the door, I saw my father lying on the bed in the fetal position, his back to me. From behind me, my mother picked me up and laid me in between them. He didn't roll over to see me; he just lay there, motionless. For about ten minutes, I lay with them and listened to them cry. I waited for an explanation of what was happening, but it never came. For the remainder of the day I would leave and return to this room, only to find them in the same position with the same look in their eyes.

One week later, I finally got the answer to my question when I watched my father get in his car and drive away to start a new life with a woman he had met at work. I stood there sobbing and calling his name from the porch. As he backed out of the driveway, I tried to make eye contact with him in hopes that he might see me and change his mind. Hysterically, I screamed at the top of my lungs when I realized he didn't see me. As he pulled forward and drove past the front of our house, I waved my hands in the air, trying to get his attention. He turned his head the other way. I could hear my mother from inside the house calling for me to come to the kitchen. Shutting her voice out of my mind, I continued to call my father back to me as he drove off into the distance. After standing there for what seemed like an eternity, I made my way to my mother, who was standing in the kitchen with a peanut-butter sandwich in her hand. She handed it to me with tears in her eyes and left me alone.

In the three minutes it took for my dad to get into his car and drive out of my life, something horrible happened deep in my heart. It was a pain that is indescribable. It felt like my heart had been put through a meat grinder. My soul was crushed that day. I've never been able to quite put it into words. Six-and-a-half-year-old boys are not equipped to wrestle for a sound mind or a will to go on living. These things are taken for granted. Having been stripped of both, I became numb and incoherent. I ran a high fever and began throwing up violently. My mother rushed me to the doctor. The doctor gave the explanation that all doctors give when this happens. He said I'd suffered a traumatic event and my reaction wasn't unusual. He told my mother to take me home and make sure I got plenty of rest.

I have often pondered looking that doctor up and suing him for malpractice. You see, if he had taken the time to check my pulse, he would have surely found the cause for my fever and vomiting. If he had put his stethoscope to my chest and listened, he would have known for certain why breathing was so difficult for me. If he had done any of these things, he would have found that I was dead.

I was dead before I came to meet my mother in the kitchen. I was dead on the way to the doctor's office, and I was dead on arrival. In fact, for the next twenty years I was a walking dead man. The only two emotions I experienced were anger and depression. Though my body continued to grow, my heart had perished within me. At the age of twenty-six, I reasoned like a six-year-old boy. My emotions were unstable and out of control. When things didn't go my way, I threw temper tantrums and annihilated anything and anyone standing in my path. My actions and reactions resembled those of a small child. Six-year-old boys destroy toys and demolish trinkets, but twenty-six-year-old men with six-year-old hearts destroy worlds and demolish lives.

Because this happened at such a young age, I did what so many hundreds and thousands of others have done. I began searching for someone to love me. My father's leaving told me that I was not worth his sticking around. I wasn't worth loving. I began a desperate effort to fill his void. I became needy and anxious when I started a relationship, and when the void came back, I'd leave and try to find love somewhere else. For more than twenty years I searched high and low for the experience that would make me whole once again. It wasn't until that day as a pastor when I fell head over heels in love with the people in my congregation that I finally realized how love works.

After going from town to town, from person to person, and from relationship to relationship in an effort to find someone to love me, I finally could see clearly how upside down my thinking was. It was not only upside down, but it was inside out, backward, and 100 percent wrong. I was defining love in the same way that most people in this generation do: by how it benefited me personally.

Imagine my surprise when I discovered that the experience of love is not in receiving it, but in *giving* it. Having someone to love you is not the same as living in love. The only way to live in love is to be the lover. True joy and fulfillment come through loving people, not through finding someone to love you. Sadly, our world and our religion have turned this upside down. We believe and teach that the experience of love is all about receiving it for ourselves. This alteration of the truth comes at a steep price. The cost is life itself.

Because each of us has truth already written on our hearts, we instinctively know that God is love. That knowing sense is the signature of the One who created us. It's the "batteries included" that comes with every human heart. This is why people who have never attended a church in their lives can know instinctively that we Christians are wrong about half the things we say about God. They already know that God is love. The problem comes when they try to identify what love is.

Because of this implanted signature on our hearts, whatever we believe about love, we believe about God. Over the years we have redefined God's heart in a way that depicts Him as being the ultimate self-seeker in the universe because this is precisely what we believe to be true of love. If this is not evidence that we've made God out to look like the devil, I don't know what is. I believe this is ultimately the reason so many people won't give their hearts to Him. Nobody likes a selfish person, and nobody likes a selfish God.

We have presented Him as caring only about His will and thinking nothing of our will. Because of this, many Christians have become terrified of things as simple as making a choice in life. They fear that the choice they make will not be the "God choice." It's as though they believe that whenever they are faced with a menu of options, there is only "one" that is in God's will and all the others are not. Some people pray and fast in an effort to know God's will, and until they feel they do know it, they just sit in fear and do nothing. I can't count the number of times I've sat and listened to sincere people talking about how literally terrified they are of being out of the will of God.

The result of this twisted theology is what I see throughout modern-day Christianity: people who have lost themselves to a religion that demands they forsake their own desires and dreams in an effort to make God happy. I have found that in this generation, people no longer have any idea what they like and dislike. Many people I've met will openly tell me that they don't even know who they are anymore because they have been trained to constantly try to be like someone else. I've watched thousands of well-meaning Christians drastically limit their dreams to fit into the institutional system they've grown up with. They're not allowed to dream outside church. Many people won't even further their educations because they've been taught that might be too self-serving.

Amazingly, we are taught that God is so self-seeking He actually requires us to bash ourselves and acknowledge our worthlessness in His presence. We think God actually desires to hear us acknowledge that "we are not worthy," or that "we are filthy and wicked." Whoever can put themselves down in the most colorfully degrading ways gets the badge of true spirituality pinned to his or her shirt.

Unfortunately, this attitude has become the politically correct way of thinking in the church today. People refuse to even receive a pat on the back for a job well done, for fear that would be stealing glory from God. All kind words and compliments are religiously rejected and redirected to God. We have come to believe that God expects us to never receive anything without reminding ourselves and everyone around us that it wasn't us, but rather it was all God.

We were trained to be the perfect girlfriend to an abusive God. Our mind-set is: "He must become greater, and we must become less." Our *selves* must be drained out and become conformed to Jesus. Our modern-day view of *Christlikeness* is tainted by a belief in a self-seeking God. We've come to see Christlikeness as the same as being Christ impersonators, and so we live in a world of competition where people do their best to impersonate their personal idea of Jesus. Sadly, many of us lose our own identity in the process. Uniqueness or individualism has become unattractive in American Christianity: God doesn't want individuals; He wants clones of Himself.

Many of us have also adopted a mentality in which we believe that everything God does in our lives has to do with some mastermind plan He has to further His kingdom. This misguided mind-set is one of the most self-seeking accusations we launch against Him. We define the Christian walk as "serving God" because we think this is ultimately what God is in it for. We think He wants an entourage of personal slaves. Anyone with a personal goal or ambition is made to feel guilty and submit to the teaching that says we don't matter. We must give up our personal ambitions for God. Our plans must become His plans, and until we submit to the "Master," we will never find true happiness. If God really requires that, He's well beyond self-seeking.

We're taught that even the gifts God has given us are to be used for His glory and only His glory. Amazingly, thousands of people have given themselves over to this "It's all about God" mentality. I cringe when I hear Christians looking toward the sky in prayer and saying, "Use me God; use me." We have truly come to believe that our God is the ultimate self-seeker in the universe.

Even the subject of sin has become tainted by this way of thinking. Many of us have been taught that when we sin, God is personally offended because He sees all sin as how it pertains to Him. When a famous evangelist has a fall, it is not uncommon for the Christian world to first mourn over how it makes God look rather than recognize the embarrassment and humiliation that this person's mistake caused himself and his family. We're taught to never sin because doing so makes Jesus look bad. We think that if we don't use foul language and abstain from drugs, sex, and a long list of other things, the people of the world will see Jesus in us and they won't be able to control themselves. They'll mysteriously find themselves saying, "I want what they have." We call it our witness, and we believe that the world will know we are Christians because we don't sin.

Out of this mind-set we now have people traveling all over the world with testimonies of how God delivered them from a life of sin. Their testimonies to the world are that they used to have a problem with pornography until they met Jesus, or they used to drink and smoke until they met Jesus. Once they met Jesus, they didn't even want to have sex anymore. This is honestly what we think will win the world to God. Today, in the minds of most Christians, Christianity is a religion about not sinning. It is my belief that we have evolved into this way of thinking because we believe in a self-seeking God who cares only about how He looks and nothing about us.

God Is Not Self-Seeking

God did not send His only Son to die because God was so offended by sin that He needed to whack someone in order to feel better. A "sin offering" is not made to God. A sin offering is an offering made to sin. Sin is a beast that wants to devour us. Imagine you are camping in the wilderness alone and you come upon a grizzly. The moment that bear sees you and begins running toward you, I promise you this: *you had better come bearing gifts!* If you have nothing to offer that beast, he will devour you. The sacrifice on the cross was essentially

Christ throwing Himself in front of the beast on your behalf and allowing it to consume Him while you escaped. Jesus did not die on the cross to satisfy God's moral rage at your sin. He died to save you from the beast of sin. The death He died, He died to sin, once and for all.

It's interesting that God gave His only Son as a ransom to set us all free from the beast of sin, and two thousand years later we have actually altered the gospel and made it out to look like the ransom was paid to God. In other words, we now believe that Jesus had to die because God was *gonna bust a cap* in someone's head over this sin issue, so it might as well have been Jesus rather than us. How touching. That just makes us all want to be adopted by that Father, doesn't it? Make no mistake about it. It was sin that devoured Jesus, not God. "The wages of sin is death." Those wages are paid to us by sin, not by God.

God is not concerned with how He looks when you fail. His concern is always about you. He is never personally embarrassed by your faults and shortcomings. His reputation means nothing to Him. It's *you* He cares about. He is just as grieved when you fall as He is when some famous evangelist falls. It's not about Him. If God were so worried about His reputation, why would He take all of your sin upon Himself and actually *become sin* in order to set you free? Think about that! God is never self-seeking.

God's loathing of sin has nothing to do with how it affects Him. He despises sin because it destroys His children. When you come to Him begging for forgiveness for something you've done, His forgiveness is not even the issue. The real issue is whether or not you can forgive yourself for sabotaging your own life. Don't think for a moment that He is offended and mortified because of what your sin *did to Him*. It's not about Him. He is in anguish because of what your sin *did to you*!

My wife and I have written an easy-to-remember poem for our children, "No doors, no drawers, no chairs, no stairs." I came up with this because I have found that these are the four most dangerous things to a child. Ninety percent of the time, when one of my children is injured, it's because they were playing with or on one of these things.

When they get hurt playing on the stairs, am I personally offended? Of course not, because it's not about me. The pain in my heart is born out of a sincere, selfless love for my children. I hate what stairs do to kids when they fall down them. This is God's heart when it comes to your sin.

God's first concern is your happiness and fulfillment. His desire is to give you abundant life. His gifts are to enhance your life and bring you the most joy possible. His kingdom is not about Him; it's about you, and it does not benefit Him one iota until He sees that you are receiving that fulfillment. Sadly, we have been raised to expect God's will and plans for our lives to be something we will naturally hate. For the most part, we can't conceive of a God who would want us to do the things our hearts desire. We've been trained to believe that God gets a kick out of calling us in the opposite direction of where we want to go, as though it's always a test to see if we will serve Him over the things we desire. Love simply does not think this way. It doesn't look to be served. Love *serves*, remember?

When we say that God wants to "use us" in some way to further His purposes, we are truly saying an awful thing about His heart. This perhaps is the most grieving thing to me when I hear people talk this way. It's as though we think He sees us as pawns in His big plan, and whatever way He can use us for His own means and purposes, He will. I cannot accurately describe to you the level to which this grieves His heart. The mere thought of it implies that God would rather have a *whore* than a wife. It is so cold and unloving, and it has nothing to do with the truth of who He is.

The gifts He has given you are never to be used at your expense. He does not want you to be used by anyone, and He will never use you. Your gifts were given to you for the purpose of bringing joy to *your* life, not for the purpose of serving Him or furthering His cause. Your happiness is His cause. If you have joy and contentment, the radiance of Christ will shine through you, and His presence and existence will speak for itself. He gets glory and is happy when you are free and at liberty. Your gifts were given for this purpose.

God is *never* envious when others admire you and love you because of your giftedness. This is the reason He gave you these gifts in the first place. He wants people to think highly of you and respect you. He loves it when folks are drawn to you and when they are amazed at how gifted you are. God is never tempted to take a gift away from you if He feels that you are receiving glory for it. He loves it when people lift you up and admire you. Every father who loves his children thinks this way.

Imagine if I bought my wife a dress that complemented her beauty and made her stand out in a crowd, and all I was concerned about was whether or not she let people know I was the one who bought it for her? What kind of husband would I be if I required her to correct people when they told her how nice she looked and inform them that she was really ugly and her husband deserved all the glory for getting her the dress? Yet, this is how we portray the heart of our God. Christians today have been trained to purposefully cover their lights, rather than let them shine for all to see, for fear that God might get angry at how bright they are. How crazy is that?

God does have a purpose, but that purpose is not for us

to be servants and messengers for Him. His purpose is for us to be His sons and daughters, and out of those relationships, *we* become the message. The problem is that we will never open ourselves to these relationships if we think He is self-seeking. That's repulsive to any thinking person. At any point where we veer from this truth, our hearts will naturally be turned away from intimacy with Him.

What is the one thing all good parents want for their children? They want them to enjoy life. If your child is not currently happy, you can accept it. If they're not yet fulfilled, you look forward to when they will be. But if they're consistently not enjoying life, it doesn't matter how clean he keeps his bedroom or how well she does in school. Nothing matters except seeing the joy and contentment come back to their faces. God's heart is the same way. He's not pleased when you're in bondage or personal anguish, and He loves you through the struggles and difficulties in your life.

Though our love for God is extremely important to Him, we also need to understand that God is not a needy love junkie. Many people try to bargain with Him by holding out their devotion like a carrot in front of His face. They use their love for Him as a negotiation tool, thinking He's as self-seeking as we are. He will never be moved or manipulated by promises of dedication and adoration. Your love must always be free, just as His is. We bargain because we believe in our hearts that God's love for us comes at a price. Make no mistake about it, God's love is not concerned with what He can get; He's concerned with what He can give. This is the essence of love, and it paints a perfect picture of His heart. Until we turn things right side up, we will continue to view God as we do the devil: selfish.

If God chose what He wanted for us and imposed His will on our every action, we'd be robots. When Adam was naming the animals, the Bible says that whatever he named them, that's what they were called. God gave that choice to Adam, and whatever Adam decided, God went along with it and blessed it. The fact that He created you and me with choice is evidence that God is "you-seeking." He waits for your choice in any situation, and once you make it, He accepts it, good or bad. He stays with you all the way, no matter what. He didn't create you to be like a car on an amusement park ride, moving around on a laid-out track without the ability to explore at will. God's will is that you use your will. He gave it to you. He delights in it. He loves the way you think and reason. Wherever you go and wherever you end up, He will be there with you. When you ask God where He wants you to go or what He wants you to do, His response is, "Where do *you* want to go? What do *you* want to do?" For many people, this fact alone carries a freedom more vast than they've ever imagined.

His Spirit will never overpower you and your choices. So don't waste time praying for God to do it. You were created in His image, and part of that image is having choice. In fact, self-control is one of the fruits of the Spirit. When His Spirit lives inside you, you'll have self-control because that's His main desire for you. Believe it or not, love desires your independence. Independence is the very foundation of free will, and your freedom is the image of God in you. If He were to try to snuff that out, He'd be degrading His own image.

The notion that God would have us put ourselves down to make Him bigger is completely wrong. In fact, from His perspective, it's heartbreaking. You'll hear this taking place in worship services across the country. How many of us believe He gets a rise out of our demeaning ourselves? Who do we think He is? What Father enjoys this? We're literally telling Him that what Jesus accomplished on the cross wasn't worth spit. We didn't get it; we're still scum. We deny the very righteousness He freely gave us and choose to proclaim its ineffectiveness in our lives. And we do it in a sense of worship, no less. This is catastrophic!

Believe it or not, when you reject someone's compliment and "give God all the glory," He doesn't receive an ounce of glory. In fact, when someone compliments God's creation, who is receiving the glory? That's right. And God is complimenting *you* as well through that. Do you think He needs or wants to hear that it was "all Him"? He's proud of you! What kind of father wants his children to reject his compliments? God is proud of you when you accomplish something, and there is *no* part of His heart that wants "all the glory." Curse the very idea.

This is one of the most self-seeking perceptions we have of Him today. We end our prayers with "We'll be careful to give *You* all the glory," as though He's checking up on us to make sure we don't steal a little for ourselves. But think of Moses coming down off the mountain after spending time with God and his face shining with glory. God had no problem with that because Moses was His boy. God's heart desires that all His glory be upon His children. He is *not* in competition with us; He is our greatest promoter. When His glory is on us, He twinkles with delight. I want my good parts to be in my children, and God is the same way with you. He may even share His glory with someone outside His family who seeks to possess it for selfish reasons! How much more is He pleased to bathe you in that glory?

People think this way because they haven't crossed over into the New Testament world. Everything is different now because of what Christ did! We are now family members. Until this foundational New Testament fact is understood, we will always be stuck in an Old Testament "hired hand" way of thinking. It's imperative that God's heart now be viewed as a Father's and not a dictator's. Fathers are not self-seeking!

Be aware also that becoming Christlike is not a process in which we train ourselves to "impersonate" Jesus. Becoming Christlike is the process by which we allow the same essence that motivated and drove Jesus to also drive us in life. It's the essence of Christ—His character, not His personality or mannerisms.

Elvis impersonators do what they do at a steep price. Many literally lose themselves in the process of trying to become Elvis-like. The sad thing is that none of them has an ounce of Elvis in them. If they did, they certainly wouldn't be impersonating him in Las Vegas. They would be leading a whole new revolution and inspiring a generation to think for themselves. To be Elvis-like is not to look, dress, act, and sound like Elvis Presley.

The inner workings of the heart made him who he was. People like John Lennon and Jimmy Hendrix were "Elvis-like," in my opinion. Though they never looked or sounded like Elvis, they had the heart and drive of a revolutionary. This is essentially what being Christlike is about: being driven by the same power that drove Christ, namely love.

God isn't in heaven saying, "Why can't you be more like Jesus?" Instead, He looks at us and says, "I'm so glad you're becoming more like *you*!"

When we understand that love is others-seeking and not self-seeking, we begin to see the heart of our Father. And if He isn't self-seeking, it's a hundred times easier to believe that He could not be easily provoked, which is the subject of our next chapter.

CHAPTER 10

The Angry God?

As the garage door was closing and my parents could be heard backing out of the driveway, the excitement in the air began to rise. My youngest brother, Brian, was peeking through the living room window, ready to give the signal the moment they drove out of sight. As soon as the coast was clear, the fun began.

The six of us kids had created a game with our family dog that I am almost embarrassed to tell you about. His name was Pierre. He was a French poodle, and he had the nastiest temper I had ever seen. Because of the fact that he was a poodle, it made it all the more fun to provoke him to anger. The last creature one would expect to act so bold would be a French poodle. We found it hilarious. Plus, we just had to do it because—you know—he was a poodle.

I suppose if he had been a German shepherd or a rottweiler, we wouldn't have played such a game, but Pierre could do nothing more than chase us around the room and snip at our heels. French poodles can't even snap; they snip, and Pierre was the worst-tempered, snippiest dog on the block. If dogs could have a short man's complex, he definitely would have had it.

In the corner of the living room sat a crushed velvet chair that had flaps that draped to the floor. Pierre would hide under the chair (in absolute fear) while one of us would go around behind the chair. The other five would run around in circles in the middle of the room, screaming like maniacs. The kid behind the chair would tilt it backward without warning, and Pierre would dart out and snip the heels of whoever was closest. It was kind of like "musical chairs," only with an angry poodle instead of chairs.

Over and over we did this, and every time that dog came snipping, the sounds of children screaming filled the house. We were careful to give each child a turn as the "chair tilter" so that everyone could experience the exhilaration of provoking Pierre. By the time we heard the garage door opening again, this poor dog was on the verge of a heart attack. Seconds later my parents would walk into a living room full of children diligently doing homework and playing a quiet board game while Pierre was in the corner making that coughing noise that sick dogs make. I thank God to this day that Pierre couldn't speak English. Our parents would have put us in therapy for years for doing such a thing. Actually, if Pierre could have spoken at all, I'm quite sure he would have been in therapy.

It would be too easy to reduce the subject of this chapter to "anger" alone. Though it is true that love is not easily provoked to anger, the fact is, love is not easily provoked to anything. Love cannot be moved from one emotion to another. It cannot be content and happy in one moment and be hurled into anger, depression, happiness, or offense the next. Love is stable and real, and it cannot be controlled.

The issue here is really control. There is a term in our society that baffles me. It's a label we put on people who constantly seek to control others. We call them "control freaks." While there are many people who are controlling and overbearing, I am amazed that *they* are the ones being called such a name. If you ask me, the people allowing themselves to be controlled are the real freaks. Why would anyone want to do this?

There is something about losing control that becomes strangely addictive. In fact, giving up self-control is the essence of addiction. This is why it is so hard to recover from things like alcoholism and pornography and drug addiction. Having no control becomes a convenient pattern of life, and the prospect of regaining self-control feels almost unnatural. It takes too much personal responsibility. It requires us to stand on our own two feet and be accountable. It is much easier to lie back and allow others to control us. It doesn't take any work.

Our view of love in this generation has been so distorted that we actually expect a loss of control to come over us when we are in love. In fact, love has been turned, tied, and twisted around so much that we now call it "*falling*" in love. We actually relieve ourselves of all personal responsibility. It's looked upon as an accident that was unavoidable, and those to whom it happens are not to blame. It's not surprising to see that people who subscribe to this mentality often "fall" out of love as quickly as they "fell" in love. After all, accidents happen, and whom can you blame when love is involved?

It's amazing to see how often my own children test the waters with me in an effort to routinely reevaluate the stability of my love for them. To put it simply, they provoke me. They purposefully edge their foot across a line that I've set for them while glancing my way to see my reaction. Will I lose my temper? Will I scream at them? Will I just sit there and do nothing? What will I do?

They're testing me to see what my limits are. What they are really doing is checking to see if there is any point of control they might gain over me. They want to know if their actions can manipulate my behavior. If I lose my temper, they are the ones who gain that control over me. If I sit there and do nothing, they have established that they can override my rules for their lives without any consequence. From a very early age until the present, they have tested me to see where I stand.

I have watched families in which a three-year-old child has complete control over his mother and father. It's almost comical to observe. Psychologists tell us that it's just the child starving for attention, but I don't think it stops there. I honestly believe that the child is starving for control. Many children play their parents like a fiddle. The parents are so provoked by them that the child literally decides the mood of the home moment by moment. The parents become like puppets in the child's hands. Whatever the child wants to happen can be manipulated into existence simply because the mother and father are easily provoked. At the end of the day, both parents blame their love for their child as the reason they were provoked by him so easily.

The downside of this game is that while "little Billy" may be able to control his parents, Billy also has an unavoidable inner sense that parents who are provoked are parents who don't love. Children need stability in their parents. Just like the rest of us, they have the truth of love written on their hearts, and that truth is that *love is not easily provoked*. Ironically, they test it and try it, but that child needs his parents to stand strong and not be controlled. The moment the parents cave in to manipulation, intimacy is put off another day. Children will not give their hearts to mothers or fathers they can control. There is no security in that. They need something bigger than a *screaming, angry daddy* or a *sobbing, worried mother*. Children are looking for something bigger than they are, and until they find it, they will never share their true selves. This is why kids who can provoke their parents are almost always blatantly disrespectful to them as well.

Parents also try to provoke their children in a number

of ways. They'll use fear or shame to get their children to obey. Threats of pain and punishment are always waved in the child's face. Many times guilt is the great provoker; and with some parents, the threat of withholding love and affection does the trick. Whatever the technique, the mentality behind it is the same. It all comes from a heart that doesn't understand the truth about love.

We have become a society of broken people who have mastered the art of pushing the right buttons in others to get what we want. Unfortunately, we never feel a sense of security in any one relationship, and without that, we are empty and alone.

Some people become experts at provoking others. They are known as being "provocative." We all are familiar with this term. When we hear it, we immediately associate it with someone we know personally. You might even have a list of people who fall into this category. If you don't, just pick up any one of the thousands of women's magazines that promote provocation. Even department store catalogs are laced with it. Turn on the television and you will see it in every commercial, sitcom, and movie. We not only believe that *love is easily provoked*, but we're a nation that wants it no other way. We feed on it.

I feel bad for those women who believe love is easily provoked. This false understanding causes many to become trapped in degrading experiences and abusive relationships where they feel "loved" by men who act crazy and lose self-control. The morbid satisfaction many women derive from this kind of relationship becomes addictive, and many begin to feel they aren't loved if their men aren't easily provoked to fly off the handle at them. Some abused women admit they purposefully push their men's buttons to get that response because it's the only form of "love" they understand.

And I submit to you that this is the cracked lens through which we view God today. Sadly, we've been taught that being provocative is how to get answers to prayers. In fact, most Christians seem to believe that God simply will not move unless provoked. We've created a remote-control god who jumps into action the moment the right buttons are pushed, and many people spend their entire lives trying to figure out the correct code to punch into the God keypad so they can get what they want.

We *act out* what we think God wants to see and hear, hoping He will be fooled into reacting on our behalf. Some people even speak in Bible verses when talking to Him because they think it makes them sound superspiritual and God will respond. Others might try to appear to be weeping before Him or in great pain so He will feel bad and answer their prayers. It seems the majority of today's teachings on prayer are "how-to" teachings regarding provoking God.

There are many beautiful and authentic times when people sincerely wail and mourn during their prayers. When strong emotions come from a broken heart that is calling on God to bring healing and comfort, He is truly moved. However, when we're faking emotion or passion in an effort to manipulate God, we are declaring our belief in an easily provoked heavenly Father. I have found this to be the case more often than not.

We read that God desires us to enter His presence with boldness, so we act out boldness the best we know how. Then we learn that God desires us to have a humble heart, so we do our best to depict humility when we come to Him. Some of us have heard that God is a God of passion, so we throw our hands in the air and strain ourselves in an attempt to create passion. When all else fails, we do what we all have learned to do as a last resort. We quote Scripture to God in an effort to "legally" force Him to follow through with what He said He would do.

As far as many of us are concerned, God could just put heaven on autopilot and leave. We openly talk as if God no longer has a choice in any matter. We say, "If it's in His Word, He has to do it." There is something within us that thinks exactly the way our children do. We try for all we are worth to provoke, control, and force our God into doing what we want, but deep in our hearts we need Him to be stronger than us. Sadly, many Christians are taught to believe that He does give in. We are basically raised with what I call a "vending machine god." If we have faith, He has to do it. If we read a Bible verse, He has to react. If we give in the offering, He has to bless us. If we have two or three people agree on something, He has to give it to us.

In the end, we come up with hundreds of little "tools" that supposedly provoke God to act on our behalf. We come up with things like using Jesus' name, exercises intended to provoke deeper belief, and out-of-context Scripture passages in an effort to provoke Him to action. We even use giving and acts of kindness, like little buttons on our remote control. All of these methods are manipulation. They are attempts to force Him into action without actually having a relationship with Him and knowing Him intimately.

People's response to fund-raising appeals gives more evidence that we believe God is easily provoked. Watch Christian television, and you might think God would do anything for money. If the televangelists are right, I'd rather have nothing to do with Him at all.

Many of us were raised with a God of anger. And not only that, we were taught He's *easily* angered. It doesn't take much to set Him off. We quote Old Testament passages that seem to depict Him as a volcano waiting to erupt. We study passages where people were put to death and use them out of context as evidence against Him. Then we hold the threat of God's anger over the head of anyone who might be thinking of leaving the church or doing something sinful. It becomes the dark cloud that follows us wherever we go.

Not only do we believe in an angry God, we depend on His anger. He *has* to be short-tempered, or we might just go out and sin. Many Christians in America believe that we need an angry God in order to keep other people and ourselves in line. Why do those who need to believe in an angry God to motivate them to holiness sometimes react with anger toward anyone challenging their beliefs? I have watched people panic at the mere mention of this message of grace. The power they've drawn from to quit destructive habits and abstain from sin was rooted in their fear of punishment from an angry God. And when grace threatens to strip that power away, they are left with only themselves and an overwhelming fear of what they might do.

Fear has become the glue that holds the institutional church together. If ministries were to eliminate fear as a motivator, their businesses would literally cave. The infrastructure that holds them together would be gone. Our beliefs about God are laced with this same poison. Offering sermons, altar calls, Communion, and even sermons about salvation rely on fear to motivate people and "seal the deal." Amazingly, we now hear that it's *holy* to be terrified of God.

The claim that God will turn on you if you sin is dead wrong. Yet this very fear is the reason many people call themselves believers. Most of Christianity is built on the fear of hell. It's as if God has given us an offer we can't refuse: "Turn or burn!" If Christians found out hell was officially closed, how many would really choose a relationship with God?

An interesting thing I've found is that people either see

God as hostile and angry, or they see Him as depressed. The teachings I grew up with depicted the Holy Spirit as being easily hurt and offended. It didn't matter what we did; the Holy Spirit was bound to get His feelings hurt. Like many people, I learned to live in fear of hurting His feelings. God reminded me of my earthly stepfather who got a hurt, disappointed look on his face every time I did something wrong. He was the teary Native American looking down from his horse on the trash people had left on the side of the road. I always felt like I owed him a lifetime of apologies.

I remember a time I became nervous when a preacher said those infamous words: "The Spirit of God is in this room." I felt like the audience was being encouraged to be sensitive that the Spirit was there because the Spirit was so sensitive. It seemed the preacher was saying that if anyone stepped out of line or said something wrong, the Holy Spirit would get His feelings hurt and lock Himself in the bathroom and cry His eyes out in disappointment. I got to the point where I didn't even want Him to come around anymore. It was exhausting trying to spare His feelings and protect His sensitive heart.

God Is Not Easily Provoked

Make no mistake about it: *God will never turn His face from you!* His eyes are constantly on you in loving affirmation. To even say that God would turn from you is an anti-Christ mentality. It denies the work of Christ on the cross. It will simply never happen. Don't ever worry that God is not watching over you. You are everything to Him. Nothing you ever do will cause Him to be provoked and turn away from you.

Many times we confuse natural *consequences* with *withholding blessings*. If you give nothing, God will not love you any less than if you give everything you have. In the spiritual realm there are laws, and the laws that govern giving in the spiritual realm are not about blessing or lack of blessing. They're governed by natural consequences, and they apply to every human being on earth, believer and nonbeliever alike.

God is as grieved by those who try to provoke Him through counting to make absolutely sure they give the required 10 percent as He is by those who don't have "cheerful hearts." He is also grieved by those who beat themselves up because they fell short. We have been taught to expect nothing from God and that He can't bless us unless we first "pay" our tithe. This is preposterous and straight from the Old Testament.

God is not provoked when people purposefully put themselves in financially dangerous positions in the name of faith. Indeed, there are accounts in Scripture where someone was down to their last penny and when they gave it, God created a miracle. Sometimes life brings you to a place of devastation, and the promise of your Father is that when you get there He will hold you up and deliver you. Manufacturing that situation on purpose is provoking the Lord. Why take something beautiful and force it into something mechanical? He doesn't need Scripture brought up to Him, and He doesn't need to be reminded of what He said. Your Father doesn't need to be provoked into helping you; He finds personal *pleasure* continually blessing the ones He loves.

Since I fell in love with people, I've noticed there are two perspectives about what it means to be sensitive. Ironically they stand at opposite poles from each other. We call a person "sensitive" when he gets offended so easily that people have to walk on eggshells around him. Another person is "sensitive" to the needs of others. Yet both people are *sensitive* even though they're reflecting opposite definitions. I'm astonished at the number of Christian teachings that depict the Holy Spirit as being like the first definition. As a result, we've become terrified of "grieving the Holy Spirit." In fact, many people will admit that they secretly feel as if they've hurt the Holy Spirit more times than they can count.

God's Spirit is the second definition of sensitive. He is sensitive to our needs. He knows everything about us. He waits for the perfect time before speaking, and when He does, He speaks in the perfect tone and says the perfect thing.

The Holy Spirit is focused on your heart. He is sensitive because He is sensitive to *you*. Don't ever worry that you've hurt His feelings. Believe it or not, the Holy Spirit is extremely difficult to hurt because He's an amazingly secure person. You can't easily "provoke" the Holy Spirit to anger or to grief. His emotions are stable because He loves you, and love is not easily provoked.

God is not provoked with our "spiritual tools" either. When I speak my daughter Landin's name, it erupts with power the moment it leaves my lips. The essence of Landin fills the air around me. I can hear her voice the moment her name is spoken. I can feel her hair in my hands and smell her breath as if she were standing right before me. That name has power within it because of the relationship I have with that little girl. She has become all that I am. The power is in the relationship. Before I had Landin, her name meant nothing to me. It was just another name among millions. But once I knew her personally, it exploded with meaning and power.

The name of Jesus is much the same way. It was never meant to be used as a bobby pin to pick a lock in the spiritual realm, or as a clove of garlic to ward off vampires. Its power is contingent upon relationship. Only in relationship can the essence of Jesus hit the air when the name is spoken from your lips.

The same is true with faith. These things that we use as

tools were meant to be the aroma of relationship, not keys to get what you want. Believe it or not, when your name is spoken by God, it explodes with power in the same way. God does not use things like your job, your children, and your marriage as tools to manipulate you to greater performance. The power comes from relationship. Faith viewed through the lens of love and relationship will come to be more than you ever dreamed, something beautiful and life-changing. Never again will you think the same. And never again will you worry about God's being easily provoked.

CHAPTER 11

The Great List-Keeper?

One day I was in my office counseling a married couple. I was dazzling them with my "relationship wisdom," and they were visibly moved. In fact, it looked like I was going to save their marriage in one short hour. As I so brilliantly described the essence of marriage and the beauty of becoming "one," I could see that I was getting through to each of them. Little did I know that back at the homestead there was a storm brewing.

Both the man and his wife were already in tears and had made incredible breakthroughs in the short time they were in my office. Just as I was giving a heartfelt discourse on "how to live in the heart of your spouse," my phone rang. Usually I have it on "do not disturb," but occasionally I forget. I immediately apologized for the distraction. They were both understanding and encouraged me to go ahead and answer it. It was my wife.

The first words out of her mouth were, "I want a separation!"

"Excuse me?"

"I've been thinking about it, and I'm not happy in this marriage and I want a separation."

I'd heard the term "poker face" before. But it wasn't until that moment that I actually understood its innate purpose and value. With this couple sitting only three feet in front of me, I kept the straightest, most dignified face I could muster. Because of the fact that I know my wife so well, and this was 100 percent out of her character, I knew immediately that something wasn't right. I nonchalantly answered back, "Yeah, okay, we'll call you later then, bye-bye," and I hung up. I continued the counseling session (with a bit less enthusiasm than before) and respectfully sent the impressed couple on their way.

By the time I got home that night, my wife was laughing at herself because she knew what had happened. She apologized several times and explained that because we'd had our first two children back-to-back, she was in the middle of her first menstrual cycle in three years, and it came upon her like an unexpected emotional hurricane. I had already figured out what had happened, and we both had a good laugh about it, and then the incident was dropped.

This was one of those incidents in our marriage I could have saved in the back of my mind for another time. I could have brought it up to her whenever she made me angry or insecure. I could have held it over her head in an effort to get things I wanted from her. Worse yet, I could have even done the same thing to her. Before this time, divorce was never once mentioned in our marriage. Now that she had opened the door, I had full rights to threaten her with it in the midst of an argument.

I made a decision that day that I would never bring this up to be used against her for the rest of my life. I knew the future possibilities of destruction and separation that could visit us if I had not made that decision. Our relationship could have started a countdown to divorce. It was in my hands, and by the grace of God I did the right thing.

There were several reasons why I let this go. First of all,

I knew she didn't mean it. She was speaking out of an emotional frenzy and not from her heart. I knew that! I knew it because I know her. It wasn't worth holding on to something we both knew she didn't mean. Second, I dropped it because I love her so much, and I couldn't think of her carrying the regret of having "messed up" with me. The thought of that made me sick. I wanted instant freedom from that incident for her. I put that incident out of my mind fast, and we now remember it with great fondness. It's not even a dark moment.

Finally, I knew that if I held that incident over her head, she quite possibly would have repeated it every time she got the slightest bit emotional. It was imperative that I kill the possibility of condemnation quickly, or eventually it could cause the demise of our marriage.

Any time we keep a record of a wrong that someone did to us, we are imprisoning that person in a world where they will be caught in a continuous cycle of doing that same thing over and over again. This is the biggest reason most people persist in their grinding routine of sin. They have never been set free from the things of their past. The only way to set someone free is to throw away the records and give them a clean slate.

Condemnation is devastating to human hearts because it paralyzes. When someone feels condemnation, it's because they feel there's a record somewhere of what they've done wrong. Sin's power over us is in this feeling of condemnation. This line of thinking has tortured so many Christians it's difficult to know the far-reaching effects it's had on our larger faith. But condemnation is certainly why faith has come to seem more about making it to heaven than intimacy with our Father.

Years ago when one of our daughters was an infant, she

became ill. Our doctor asked us to keep a record of how many dirty diapers she had. We were religious about it. Every time she had a bowel movement we saved the diaper and put a slash on a notepad along with the exact time. After about three days of this precise documentation, I came home one evening and asked, "Where's the little poop machine?" I was defining my baby girl by the records I was keeping on her.

Obviously I was joking, but in the context of diminishing relationships by the records we keep, the concept is valid. When I talk to divorced people, it's always interesting to hear the titles they put on a former spouse. The husband might say, "She was a liar," or "She was a nagger," and the wife will tell me, "He was a workaholic," or "He was a controller." Keeping such careful accounts of the other person's faults, they began to define the person by their shortcomings. They gave the former love of their life a new name, completely forgetting the one they used before when talking with them intimately, unable to contain the joy they felt at simply saying the name.

Has our world taught us that love keeps a record of wrongs?

Many parents can't even receive a compliment about one of their children in a public setting without stepping in and correcting the person who gave it. If someone in a restaurant comments on how well behaved their children are, they feel the need to set the record straight by saying that their children are really only "acting good," and they're actually bickering brats. It's meant to be funny, but what do the listening children hear? They know what the record says about them, so they'll behave according to the name their parents call them by.

Consider the fact that when someone is in the midst of

real change in their life, their immediate family is usually their biggest discouragement. Convincing Mom and Dad that you're not the same person you were growing up is often impossible. Consequently, I commonly counsel people to create a sizable distance between them and their family during their personal change.

Possibly the greatest evidence that people believe God keeps records of their wrongs is the fact that they keep such accurate records of their own wrongs. If we really believed in our hearts that our Creator didn't keep such records, would we? Still, I've found that most people do.

It becomes a habit that won't allow any undeserved comfort to creep in and give a dose of freedom. Forgetting personal wrongs seems irresponsible or even fraudulent. Before they know it, they begin calling themselves names that correlate with the sins they've committed. People do this because they believe that in God's eyes they deserve it. Eventually, they start to believe that when they are on a personal bashing binge, it is actually the voice of God talking to their hearts like that. They'll imagine they are practicing humility by being so inwardly honest, and yet nothing could be further from the truth.

The result of this upside-down thinking is that people become "sin-focused." Their relationship with God becomes about the list of all the wrongs they've committed. Even their prayer lives are saturated with apologies and promises of purity. They end up spending so much time trying not to do certain things or attempting to break free of other things that they miss the heart of what it means to be a believer.

As I've stated, most Christians believe that God keeps a record of their wrongs because they keep records as well, not only of their own wrongs but of other people's wrongs.

They've become conformed in the image of who they believe God to be. And in many cases, it's His exact opposite, the accuser.

I am not sure that the average person has ever stopped to think about how much of their faith is based on a belief that God is a record keeper. Most of us believe our calling in life has everything to do with the mistakes we've made in our past. If a person was a drug addict in the past, he immediately thinks God will call him to minister to the drug world. If a person was a prostitute, God will surely call her to reach out to prostitutes. This is a record-keeping mentality. This perception comes from a belief that God associates our past with our future, which simply isn't true. God is not limited to or by the mistakes or problems we've had in the past.

God is in the business of restoring people, not labeling them. Look at how divorce has become the unpardonable sin in many churches. The moment someone gets a divorce, he or she is labeled for life. This is truly heartbreaking and is a result of a generation of people who believe God does keep such records.

Our belief in a record-keeping God is so pervasive, many Christians believe that if you commit "the unpardonable sin," God will never forgive you. It's perhaps the most frequent fear brought to me. This has been held over the heads of millions of people as a tool of manipulation. I remember worrying about this for the first ten years of my Christian journey. It wasn't until I understood love that I was set free from this ridiculous notion. When I had children of my own and discovered the true heart of love, I understood that nothing is unpardonable to your children. Nothing.

Our testimonies show this focus on record keeping as well. We commonly hear about the sinful things in someone's past, and yet a testimony is not about what sins you used to commit before you met God. The purpose of a testimony is to share who God is now. And this alone is powerful enough to win millions of hearts. God is not excited about what you came from; He is excited about having a relationship with you today. Out of that relationship, *you* will become a testimony.

God Keeps No Record of Wrongs

A young woman who had been married for about two years called me one day for advice. Her husband was struggling with a nasty temper, and it seemed to be getting worse every time he blew up. She explained to me that the previous night they had gotten into a disagreement and he started screaming and yelling at her. This time it did not stop with just words; he actually slapped her leg. Never before had this man gone so far as to actually strike his wife. When it was over, they were heartbroken. It was apparent to both of them that they needed an intervention.

When I sat down and spoke with this young man, he tearfully began to tell me about his mountains of failures. "I feel like I've done so many wrong things to her," he told me. "It would take years to wade through them and reclaim her heart." The more I listened, the more I realized he believed everything was such a tangled mess, he simply didn't know where to start.

His situation reminded me of my kitchen just after Thanksgiving dinner, with every plate, utensil, cup, glass, pot, and pan stacked up on the counter. The thought of even starting in on cleaning up the heaping pile of dishes makes me depressed.

Where do you start? But this is how many people feel in their relationships, even their relationship with God. They can't do the right thing until all the wrong things are cleaned up. And because we don't know where to start, we just do our best to hold things together another day until we end up repeating the same mistake and finding ourselves even worse off than before.

This man's wife eventually made a decision to "clean the kitchen" of their marriage. She did this by permanently destroying all records of his past behavior. She never brought up his past again and instead spent all her time encouraging him for the good things he did rather than reminding him of his mistakes. Once his slate was wiped clean, he knew his wife welcomed his intimacy. He began to feel that he could make the changes he knew he needed to make, and that's exactly what he did. He was driven to change through a wife who didn't keep a record of his wrongs.

Imagine a Father who does the same. He doesn't keep a record of your sins for the same reason that wife didn't keep a record of what her husband did. He doesn't want you to live with the shame and regret because He knows shame is deadly to the spirit. He wants you to let it go. Believe it or not, the only ammunition God needs against your sin is forgiveness. Coupled with your repentance, it's the only weapon that works!

Your Father doesn't keep a record of your sins because He knows if He did, you would be caged in a cycle of repetition. This is the biggest reason people continuously repeat the same mistakes over and over. They believe in their hearts that God has written down a record of their sins somewhere in heaven and He won't let it go. They've been told about the embarrassing videos of their lives that will be played back to them when they die. Because they believe this lie, they are a prisoner to the records they imagine God is keeping.

Your Father doesn't keep a record of your sins because He doesn't want anything ugly being held over your head. He is the expert record shredder. Everything He touches becomes like new. There is no such thing as an "unpardonable sin" when you're in the family. This particular Scripture applied strictly to the Pharisees who were trying to discredit Jesus by knowingly attributing His works to the devil. They were nonbelievers, not Christians. While we are at it, I would also like to state that I don't believe suicide earns a person a guaranteed one-way ticket to hell. Most Christian denominations preach this, and not one of them has scriptural proof of their opinion. Yes, suicide is a terribly selfish act that destroys many lives, but that does not mean it guarantees hell.

You are precious to Him, and when He looks at you He sees only the picture of His perfect creation. He doesn't want anything unholy or unattractive to appear in that picture. Imagine writing down the sin that one of your children committed against you on a piece of paper and then holding it over his or her head. This would be labeling your own child. When you love, this is the last thing you would ever want to do. God is no different. He is the loving Parent who is constantly wiping your face clean and fixing your hair before a family picture. He wants you to always look your best, regardless of where you have been or what you have done.

God also doesn't define your future by your past. He has no record of your past, so your future is free and clear. Though many people may have a special heart for others who have come from their previous lifestyle, this does not mean everyone is called to have a ministry that pertains to their past. Your purpose may have nothing to do with the life you used to lead, because your Father has no record of it in heaven.

It is God's desire that you let go of your past. He doesn't need you to make sure everyone knows how bad it used to be. He has truly let every wrong thing in your past go. In fact, He has cast it into the sea of forgetfulness. Believe it or not, God doesn't even refer to you as a "sinner, saved by grace," like so many Christians proudly proclaim. This, once again, is a mentality born out of the belief that God keeps records of past wrongs. He sees you as perfect forever! If you, Jesus, and Billy Graham were to stand before God to see who was the cleanest and most perfect, God would declare to you that you're all the same.

Further, God does not label people "divorced" because it's not the action He has a problem with. He hates emotional walls and the willful decision to be emotionally hidden and unknown. The sin of divorce is the divorce from intimacy and oneness that couples allow to take place in their marriages long before the legal papers are filed. Sadly there are millions of self-righteous married people in the church who don't realize they are as guilty as the people at whom they point their fingers.

God is not impressed or more predisposed to bless you because you've come so far in your spirituality. He's proud of you because you are *His child*. He loves you because you are His child. His heart for you is because of your position in His family, not because you follow the rules well and don't sin as much as you used to.

God does not bless us for being good little boys and girls. God blesses us because God blesses. When you receive a blessing from Him, just accept it and know that it's because you are His child. Believe it or not, God doesn't even keep records of what you do right. He doesn't need to. He doesn't need a reason to love you and bless you. Because you are in His family you can know for sure that His grace is extended to you forever, irrespective of what you do.

This is the truth of God's heart. He is not a keeper of records, and the more we know the source of love, the better and freer we will become.

CHAPTER 12

The Terrible God?

I was fully relaxed, lying in my bed in pitch darkness listening only to the sound of a gentle breeze running through the tree outside my bedroom window. My mind had relaxed, and I was moments away from a deep sleep. Suddenly my bedroom door was kicked open with a loud bang. Someone holding a flashlight shined it in my face, blinding me. As my eyes regained focus, I saw a man in black coming down on me with a twelve-inch French knife. I screamed in horror as adrenaline rushed through me. There was nothing I could do. There was no time to respond. The fear was stronger than any drug I'd ever experienced. When my brother got up and turned on the bedroom lights, we lay there together and laughed hysterically.

"Okay, it's my turn now," Brian said, handing me the knife and the flashlight. "Make sure you wait a long time before you come in."

"Get real relaxed, and try to fall asleep," I said as I turned the lights back off and closed the door behind me.

After about fifteen minutes of silence, I would kick the door in and reenact the same murder scene. Over and over we took turns playing the helpless victim, and each time we found it more thrilling and exhilarating than the last.

Playing the part of the attacker wasn't why we got a big

charge from this. It was the rush of fear as the victim. That was what we were after.

This was a game my brother and I stumbled upon almost twenty years ago when we lived together in Hollywood. We were two single men (is it any wonder why?) bored out of our minds and looking for something to pass the time. Since we'd already bought BB guns and destroyed every drinking glass, mug, and dinner plate in the apartment, we were running out of options.

Later we realized we were flirting with fear, hell's biggest weapon against people. And we were using it for a cheap adrenaline rush. What was so surprising to us was the power and thrill it provided when tampered with in a controlled environment. We were able to transfer something truly terrible into a world where it did not belong. I believe that this is exactly what we've done with love.

It's amazing the deep blindness we've learned to live with. The thing we've come to accept as "love" makes me think of a number of documentaries I've seen where people in distant countries eat maggots or roaches and refer to them as delicacies. In poverty-stricken countries, there may be no choice but to eat what's available. In other countries, though, people eat this stuff because they like it. They actually believe it's a special treat. When a person grows up calling diseased pests "delicacies," they get used to it over time. They learn to crave it over normal food. This is the kind of deceit we've believed about love. We've exchanged true love for maggots and roaches. And we don't even know we've done it.

We've become people who delight in evil. Most of us have never had a relationship without it. In fact, evil is the biggest portion of the attraction in many relationships. In my lifetime hundreds of women have described to me an unexplainable magnetism they felt for "bad boys," rebellious and angry men who had closed their hearts off to love. They prayed and prayed for God to reveal His perfect choice of a man to them, but they weren't attracted to such a man. Their hearts were crying out for maggots and roaches.

Consider the fact that today we can call sex between two people who don't even know each other "making love." Love doesn't call evil love. Because our world doesn't even know what love is anymore, it's easy to confuse the two.

If a married couple still lust for each other after several years, we consider them as having a healthy sex life. But love and lust are actually opposites. Love *gives*; lust *takes*. Love comes from the heart. Lust is of the flesh. Most people can't tell the difference between the two because the mechanics seem the same. The difference, however, is worlds apart. A couple who lust eventually lose interest in each other. A couple who love never lose interest. Lusting people think about pleasing themselves. Loving couples are in it for the other person.

Until we can rightly divide evil from love, we will always unite them. As long as the lines are blurred, our perception of God's heart will follow suit. This is also what's happened in our understanding of giving back to God. Modern Christian teachings appeal to the flesh, talking about giving to receive something back from God. This evil way of thinking is actually encouraged in churches where people talk of a "seed faith" offering so they can receive something back from God. We say it so flippantly that we don't even feel its deadly barbs when it latches on to our hearts. Giving to get is selfishness, pure and simple.

When I fell in love with people I began to see that at every turn we not only embrace evil, but we rejoice in its presence as well. Religion delights in making God look evil. If we ask

God to pillage the wicked on our behalf, we're declaring our belief that God is a thief. I've heard this in supposedly Christian prayers.

Others will pray for God to bring disaster and tragedy to a "backslider" or a nonbeliever so that person will realize how much they need God. Does this sound a bit off to you? People who pray this way must believe God has the heart of the devil. It's silly, and it misrepresents God.

We all have heard people quote the Scripture "Vengeance is mine; I will repay, saith the Lord." Perhaps you've even said it yourself. When someone makes us angry and we want them to pay, this is our way of imagining that God will make them pay for us. We believe God is a mafia leader who pops others who get out of line. I've seen people actually get excited when they think God has gotten back at someone on their behalf. We've turned Him into a pit bull that attacks anyone who looks at us cross-eyed. Make no mistake about it: this is evil and it has nothing to do with love.

Out of this mentality come many more terrible teachings, some that suggest God will cause something terrible to happen to us to "get our attention," or to "get us to get serious about our faith." Many people look to the sky when something bad happens and ask, "Why, God?" We believe He causes our calamities because we've been taught that love delights in evil. We've been immersed in a religion that uses fear tactics to get people to convert. This is the misguided manipulation spiritual leaders use when they boldly announce that God is punishing America with famine, sickness, and terrorism.

One of the most common fear tactics is about the idea of the future rapture of believers. Many people have been told they'll be "left behind" if they aren't ready when Jesus returns. It's held over their heads with threats and insinuations that our Father might abandon us if we aren't "ready." This is one of the most evil tactics I see used today, promoted by a religious system that not only delights in evil, but uses it as a tool for supposed spiritual growth. Christians who fear Jesus' return have been lied to by a negligent church.

Another symptom of our delight in evil is in people's reveling in their evil past before they found God. They believe the more evil they show their past to be, the more glory God gets for saving them from it. Some people's past gets worse and worse every time they tell it. I can remember as a child listening to these stories and thinking that I'd never be asked to speak publicly unless I had a long list of evil things I had done. The more evil your past, the more speaking engagements you'd get in the Christian world. Love does not delight in evil, but Christians do. And because of this, thousands of people are terrified of a God they suspect will destroy their livelihood or family to prove a point.

God Does Not Delight in Evil

God does not delight in fear tactics. Love simply never thinks this way. When we use fear either to convert people or to get them to follow the rules, we are partnering with evil. *All fear is evil.* God does not delight in the use of evil to manipulate His children into salvation or repentance.

Instead, the kindness of God leads people to repentance. He will never bully anyone into doing what He wants them to do. He doesn't use evil to fight evil, and He certainly doesn't delight in prayers that suggest He will perform evil. There is a power in love that can soften the hardest heart and bring the dead to life. The reason we resort to using fear and evil is because we don't believe love is enough. We've never encountered authentic love. We're ignorant of its power. We see love as one of several things of use in religion. And yet in *relationship*, love is *everything*.

Threats of hell were never meant to be the argument that drew people to God. The Bible says that the Holy Spirit draws us to God. Threats of hell bring fear and condemnation. Only a loveless person could think of such a thing. If someone told our children that we might abandon them if they didn't mind us, wouldn't we be enraged? It's unthinkable. We adore our children. Yet this is common practice in many Christian circles.

God finds no delight when people believe He might take one of their children or destroy their business if they don't give their lives to Him. While it may cause people to respond, they will also shrink back from God's heart. God didn't create men to save their souls from hell. He created men and women to have relationships with one another and with Him. Fear tactics make that impossible. The end does *not* justify the means. Yes, God does work through life's tragedies, but contrary to modern-day teachings, He's never the one who causes them. His promise is that in the midst of life's hardships, He will be there to comfort and heal. Even when those hardships are caused by our own actions! God never delights in people getting what they deserve. He is about saving us from what we deserve.

If a drug addict breaks into your home and steals your television for drug money and gets away, God exacts "vengeance" by taking that man out of addiction and freeing him to live his life in the knowledge of love. God's vengeance is *never* on people; it's on the devil. God does not delight in getting revenge on people, and He never participates in it. God delights in forgiveness. And when you forgive someone, you're freeing that person to receive a touch from God that will release him from hell's grip. Our battle isn't against flesh and blood—and neither is God's.

Nothing about the evil of our past glorifies God. God desires what is true, holy, pure, lovely, and of good repute. He would much rather you talk truthfully about what you have with Him *now* than who you were before. It isn't that He's secretly hoping we'll skip over the details of our lives before Him. Leaving out details for the sake of making Him look good is false advertising. Unfortunately, thousands of people won't have anything to do with God now because they're either terrified of Him or they believe false things about Him. We shouldn't try to sell God; He can stand on His own.

What if before I married my wife I sent a friend to tell her that if she didn't marry me I'd be "very disappointed" and set about messing up her life? She may agree to marry me out of fear, but she'd never give me her heart. What kind of marriage would that be? God wants people to love Him for Him, not so they can escape hell. He will never threaten our families or our health in an effort to coerce us into a relationship. When we win people with the power of fear, we make them "sons of hell," not sons of God. Using fear only proves that we haven't personally experienced a goodness that exceeds our faith in hell's evilness.

The only way to understand God's heart is to love people. When I give my daughters a gift, I don't ask God to bless me because I gave. When I present my wife with a new dress, I don't tell her I'm "giving it to her in faith" that she'll be good and do what I ask. That would break her heart. She wants to know that I gave it to her because I love her.

In Old Testament times, spiritual realities were shown in the physical realm. In New Testament times, spiritual things are played out *in the heart*. In the Old Testament, people received a physical blessing *after* they gave. Now, giving creates a blessing in the heart. If we don't love, we will always be drawn back to the "What's in it for me?" mentality. The new covenant with God must be understood through the eyes of love. God never gives for the purpose of receiving. He gives because He is love, and love gives.

Contrary to many popular teachings, God doesn't plunder people or rob the wicked. He blesses them. When we tell stories that seem to show God doing such things, we misrepresent the truth of His heart. He will never do this. He loves the atheist as much as He loves you. He sent His Son to die for the entire world. Christ died for sinners. He didn't plunder them. This is His heart. He will never abandon His own children.

Several years ago I was at the park with my children, watching them roll around in the sand and climb the jungle gym. When it was time to leave, I called their names and waved my arms. My oldest daughter kept swinging. After calling several more times, I began walking toward the car. "See ya later, Landin! We're leaving!" I shouted back at her. I will never forget the shriek of horror as she jumped down and ran to me. How many parents have done this? But just then the Lord reminded me of all the times people made me believe my heavenly Father would do that if I didn't behave exactly as He wanted. I have never again done that to one of my children.

All New Testament references to the Rapture were to encourage Christians to look forward. Never were they used to terrify people into repentance. Only now do we do this. Imagine being with the people you love most in this world on the happiest day of your life. And just before you go to meet your loved ones, someone comes and informs you that they're hiding in a broom closet because they're afraid of your coming. Would you want to come for that? Until we understand who God is, this is what we're doing to Him.

Imagine having no friends at school. All the kids make

fun of you, and even teachers humiliate you in front of the class. Then, in the midst of that, you remember, "My daddy is picking me up today, and he will make it all better." That's what God hopes for us to feel about Him.

You need to know right now that if you have ever opened your heart to God, you are safe. Nothing you do will make you any more ready. You are going with Him when He comes because you are His child. Nothing you do will ever cause Him to leave you behind. Don't let anyone tell you anything different. The Rapture was never meant to be used against you; its purpose is to encourage you.

Can you imagine someone going to your child's elementary school and standing before the kids to tell them that their parents might abandon them if they step out of line? How would that make you feel as a parent? How do you think God feels when someone does this to His children? The only way anyone could do such a thing would be if they didn't have love in their hearts. When you love, something so awful is inconceivable. Yet this is what's threatened every day in many Christian circles, and it breeds insecurity in people's hearts.

The nature of love is that it expands. All things of God expand. Living together without a promise of absolute security requires an intentional constraint on the heart. Because love comes from the heart, nonsecure relationships ultimately restrict the heart from growth until it dies. Much as a fish grows only to the size of the tank he's in, if you don't believe your relationship with God is secure, your relationship with God can't grow. Without an unbreakable covenant, you're merely "living together" with God, and your spiritual fulfillment will be stunted.

Security is free, open space all relationships need to grow. You have that in God. Don't allow anyone to tell you different. Your relationship with God and your security with Him can never be taken from you. The moment you lose sight of your security, you will cease to grow spiritually. God calls it a *promise*, and you can believe that.

The starting point of all true relationships is the knowledge that we will never be abandoned—our experience of love will never be taken away for any reason. This is the foundation of relationship with God and, therefore, the very foundation of faith. Yet sadly, millions of Christians haven't crossed the starting line of faith because they've been convinced they can lose God's love and acceptance.

My friend, you must believe in unconditional love if you want a true relationship with God. What other kind of security is there if it's not total and absolute? Anything less than that is no security at all. We give it to our children without a thought—why wouldn't God, who created us, give the same as our "Father"?

Love is the author of forever covenants. And when you truly love someone unconditionally and with all your heart, you see things in them they themselves can't even see. Our next chapter shows another thing only love can show us.

CHAPTER 13

The Condemning God?

She had watched him with a secret crush for nearly a year before they spoke. Their first conversation was nothing more than a simple hello, but to her it was a moment frozen in time. Though it wasn't a real dialogue, she had waited patiently for this moment, and it proved to be everything she had dreamed it would be. *Finally*, she thought to herself. *He knows I exist.*

Now that the door was open, she made it a priority to find herself in his company as often as possible. If a group of people was going to dinner after the church service, and he would be there, she was sure to attend. It didn't matter if they sat together; just being in the same room with him was a delight. They might exchange a glance or two, and if she was lucky, he might tell her good-bye at the end of the night.

Over the next several months, another milestone was crossed. He greeted her *by name*! He actually remembered her name. *Why would he take the time to memorize my name if he wasn't interested?* she thought. He had never asked her what her name was. Did he investigate and find out through a mutual friend? Whom could he have talked to? Perhaps he heard someone call her and he remembered. *Nevertheless, he did remember it*, she reasoned. *And that must mean something.*

On one occasion, they were hiking up a mountain at

a church retreat, and he turned and asked about a specific situation at her workplace that she'd mentioned almost six months ago. *He was listening!* she thought. Now it was becoming obvious: he was interested in her. Taken alongside the fact that he picked up her napkin when she dropped it in the dining hall earlier, things were looking good.

After that, she sits up all night with her best friend and begins recalling every incident where he showed interest. There was the time he laughed at a joke she made. Then there was the time he said he'd keep a family situation of hers in prayer. There was also the famous "poke-on-the-shoulder incident" when he wanted her attention. And who could forget the time he told her he thought he saw her driving on Bell Road and Greenway? He obviously was thinking of her during his day.

At any moment, he was sure to ask her for a date. Even if he didn't, they were already "kind of dating." She talked and talked about him until her friends got tired of hearing his name in every conversation. But she just couldn't stop herself. She knew they were supposed to be together. It was just a matter of time before it happened. If they knew him like she did, they would understand. Even her best friend was starting to come around and see the signs.

Her sister frantically encouraged this woman to come to my office. She reluctantly agreed. And in the first few seconds, his name came spilling out of her mouth. I asked her about that and her eyes got that far-off look as she shared every dazzling moment they'd had together. I'd not heard they were dating, so I was a bit taken by surprise. When I asked her how long this had been going on, she gave me a step-by-step explanation. After only a few minutes of this, it was obvious the relationship was all in her mind.

"Does he like you?" I asked.

"Oh, yes, it's obvious," she said. "I can't believe you haven't heard."

I took a more direct approach. "Did he tell you that he likes you?"

"Well, no, not in those exact words. But I know for a fact that he does."

"Has he told anyone else that he likes you?"

"He doesn't really talk to a lot of people about his feelings," she said, starting to look a bit nervous. "But if you ask my best friend, she'll tell you."

As I reached over my desk, I picked up the phone and said, "Better yet, I'll call him and ask him myself."

"*No!*" she shrieked back. "Just forget it. Forget I said anything."

I suggested that I could ask him in a way that he'd never know she'd put me up to it. No. I promised her complete secrecy, even suggesting we call a friend of his who was sure to know the truth. But she adamantly refused each suggestion.

She didn't want the truth. She preferred the fantasy.

My heart broke for this poor woman, because I knew her world was about to crash in on her. She'd lived in the most extraordinary fantasy world for almost two years, and today it was being exposed for lies. There's no easy exit for someone who has gone through this. Living a lie can feel a thousand times better than facing the truth, especially when countless hours have been spent concocting the illusion. It becomes a mysterious, romantic world where everything fits together and creates the greatest romantic story ever. This young woman walked out of my office and proceeded to re-create the same fantasy world over the next year and a half until the guy eventually married someone else.

Ironically, this pattern of behavior does not stop when

a woman like this finally does get married. Her new husband can proclaim his love to her over and over, but she will retreat into an emotional world where she imagines it's not true. Every move he makes will be misconstrued as evidence that he's thinking of leaving her. It's not so much the fantasy she is addicted to; it's her inability to recognize truth. Truth, to a fantasy-addicted person, appears boring and simple. Its plainness is a disappointment.

Women certainly aren't the only ones who do this in relationships. The only difference is that when men do this, we don't call them "dreamers," but by the more affectionate term "stalkers."

Authentic truth poses a terrible threat to our way of life in America. Our national infrastructure is built on a foundation of lies. We buy things with money we don't have, create Facebook "friends" out of people we don't even know, and expect to be lied to every time we turn on the television. Advertising makes promises to our flesh that could not possibly be fulfilled. Telling people what they want to hear is the best way to sell something. We've become so addicted to how the lies make us feel, we don't even want the truth anymore. When just the right lie is offered, it's euphoric. We feel empowered, enlightened, soothed, and even godlike. Whether or not it is true is almost beside the point.

Make no mistake: we know the claims are fantasy. We simply choose to overlook that fact. The woman who came to my office was not blindsided by these lies. She made them up herself. She knew the truth; she just refused to accept it. I've found that we almost always know the truth; we simply close our hearts off to it. It doesn't compare to the fantasy. And when carried over to our ideas of God and love, this becomes a huge problem.

A man once came to me for advice concerning a married

woman he was "in love" with. This man had rationalized his way into believing that the woman was going to leave her husband, though she hadn't agreed to that at all. I asked if he'd like to discover the truth about that. He hesitated for a moment and then asked me how. I told him to break up with her and tell her that even if she did leave her husband, he would never see her again. If three months went by and she still left her husband, then he could go back to dating her with my blessing. Needless to say, this man did not take my advice because he knew the truth already. About six months later, he did finally break up with her, only to find that she never left her husband and is still with him today.

After years of counseling, I have found that every relationship that ends in a breakup has one thing in common: the reason for the breakup came about because of something that was evident in the beginning but consciously overlooked. We're never surprised when our world of lies blows up. Though we lived the lies, we knew the truth all along. As long as we're on to feeling that dreamy feeling again soon, we'll let just about anything slide. The *romance* of the fantasy is the name of the game, and no more so than when it comes to love.

Romance is defined as "a strong, sometimes short-lived attachment, fascination, or enthusiasm for something"; "a dreamy, imaginative habit of mind; a disposition to ignore what is real"; not based on fact; "imaginary" or "fictitious"; "fanciful"; "marvelous"; "extravagant"; unreal (Dictionary.com).

It's not surprising to find that what we consider the heart of love today is actually an outright lie. We've been taught to long for untruthfulness at the very conception of relationships. This is catastrophic.

When women desire a romantic man to sweep them off

their feet, many are figuratively saying, "I want a man who will lie to me." Romance has become a game of fantasy and manipulation to gratify the flesh. We all know romance isn't reality, but we desire it because it feeds our flesh. Many times, it's innocent fun that can easily become an addiction to fantasy.

A man who is charming can get many things from women. Women dream of being "charmed" by a cunning man. Love stories and romance novels are packed with charming men who seduce women. It seems innocent enough, but look at the meaning behind it.

To charm means to cast or seem to cast a spell on; bewitch; to use magic spells; to subdue, control, or summon by incantation or supernatural influence; to affect by magic; to overcome by some secret power, or by that which gives pleasure; to allay; to soothe.

Many women are completely addicted to this form of manipulation. It provides a high that's hard to beat. And, as with most addictions, the end is a string of failed relationships and broken hearts. Should we be surprised such devastation follows trickery?

Because we have learned to romanticize love, we end up romanticizing God. Modern-day churches create hype and disperse it to sell people on God. Some promises I've heard from the pulpit about Christian life are plain lies that appeal to the flesh.

Instantaneous deliverance from sickness, a life without struggle, and financial prosperity are just a few of the charming things I've heard presented to desperate people. We think God wants us to tell the world what they want to hear in order to win them over, so we give Him an accent, a dozen roses, and a stack of winning lottery tickets to get up onstage and *sell, sell, sell!* Many churches have creative experts for selling what I call "spiritual pornography." It's a false, superficial spirituality geared toward tantalizing the carnal nature. It sells extremely well, but once you've signed on the dotted line, you find it's useless.

When we promise people all their problems will go away the moment they ask Jesus into their hearts, we're setting them up for disappointment. It happens to people every day, but in my twenty years of ministry, I have yet to hear someone share this testimony in a church. I suspect it takes years (and possibly a lifetime) to recover from the guilt and condemnation of not being able to produce what was promised in the sales pitch. I've found that Christians will admit they felt charmed into a religion that never lived up to its promises, yet they still feel compelled to fake it so no one will know it's not working for them the way it supposedly is working for others.

When we invite our neighbors to dinner for the purpose of inviting them to church, we're not acting in love. Many Christians are encouraged to become deceitful and calculating in search of new converts. Such a mind-set sidesteps love and often relies on cunning wit and manipulation. With our skewed perception of love, it's no wonder we are confused about God's heart. Do we believe that God rejoices in truth? How could we? Most of our lives are spent listening to lies about Him from superspiritual leaders who claim to be experiencing Him on levels we can only dream about.

But here is the truth. Are you ready? Superspiritual people will never find God on the path they're taking. You know the kind of person I'm talking about. They're a dime a dozen. They're not human; they're superhuman. Every facet of their humanity has been burned up by their mystical ideas of true spirituality. They float through life with a glassy-eyed distant gaze in their eyes, and all normalcy and reality have been abandoned for something "deeper." These people truly believe that the truth of God is found in rejecting their humanity and embracing their idea of mystical spiritual enlightenment. I call them spiritual porn addicts; they can't see the truth of God because the foundation of their beliefs is based on lies.

Sadly, I've rarely seen anyone addicted to this form of accentuated spirituality recover to find contentment with truth. Almost always, when a spiritual porn addict is faced with the truth about who Christ is and how spirituality really works, he's disappointed and turned off. His experience with God is usually based on fantasy, and because of his commitment to embellished spirituality, he becomes blinded to God's true heart.

Here's another shot across the bow: the number one reason so many people miss God is because they're looking too deeply. They want something huge and spectacular, and they won't accept anything less. Their hearts crave revelation beyond a dirty, homeless carpenter. They find themselves studying the Greek and Hebrew words in the Bible and looking carefully in between each line in an effort to find something deeper than what is plainly stated. They will read it over and over, waiting for a deep spiritual explosion to give them that much-needed rush they've become addicted to. And when they are finally faced with the real Christ on a lowly donkey, telling them to deny this superiority they're so attached to, it's a colossal letdown.

The Pharisees were this way in their time. They were the experts in deep revelation about God; however, when God came and stood right in front of them, they didn't recognize Him from Adam. Instead of rejoicing with the Truth (Jesus), they despised Him. They couldn't fathom accepting anything less than their lofty superspiritual fantasies about who God was. Surely, He was more profound than a simple carpenter!

Jesus Christ was a complete letdown to the religious leaders of His time. And very little has changed since then.

Today, we describe the Messiah in the same high terminology the Pharisees used in their day. Do we not reject the humble Carpenter every bit as much as the people who first met Him? Religion doesn't rejoice in the truth about Christ; religion hides it. We embellish and exaggerate and accentuate the truth the best we can in order to sell Him to the world. But He isn't the high and lofty fantasy we've concocted. He's far more.

We want to believe that God rejoices in truth, but strangely enough, when I ask anyone if God rejoices in the truth about them, they almost always cringe. We are taught that the truth about us is B-A-D. We're even encouraged to abandon our hearts for His because there's nothing good in them. This is spiritual castration, and it's encouraged the moment someone joins the faith. We are bombarded with Scriptures about how evil our hearts are and how we should never trust them because "the heart is deceitful." Once we buy into this nonsense, we begin to behave like a castrated dog. We become docile and obedient and a thousand times less likely to think for ourselves and consider the truth beyond what we'll find in this kind of church. It's a fine teaching if obedience is what you're after. But when spiritual procreation is needed, you end up with a bunch of impotent and sterile followers. And sadly, we accept this willingly because we're told that God doesn't rejoice in the truth about us.

Think about that for a moment. If you are like most people, you probably believe that God knows the truth about you and He's repulsed by it. You think this because you're certain He's kept track of where you've been and what you've done. Those things repulse you personally, so how can God think any differently?

God Rejoices in the Truth

God rejoices in the truth about you because it's truly some-thing to rejoice about. Do you believe you know the truth about yourself? What most people think is the truth is not. Religion has taught us to confuse the facts of our lives with the truth about ourselves. You are not your sin. In God's eyes, the two are as far apart "as the east is from the west" (Ps. 103:12 NKJV). The truth about you has nothing to do with what you have done or where you have been. God's eyes are fixed on the truth, and He rejoices in it because it's beautiful.

God has taken your heart of flesh and given you a new heart of love. He has made you a new creation. He delights in your heart because it's good! You can trust your heart. Life with God is lived out through the heart. What sense would it make for you to reject your heart when you ask Jesus to live in it? Your Father rejoices in your heart, and He's grieved when you talk as if it's deceitful and ugly. Your heart is the place He has chosen to live, and now your heart is connected to His forevermore.

I received a call from a pastor who was at his spiritual wits' end. This poor man had been secretly struggling with a pornography addiction and was terrified to approach anyone in the church for help. He began to tell me how terrified he was of anyone finding out the "truth" about who he really was. His statement caused me to sit up in my chair, overcome with dismay and grief for him. I asked how he felt just after he'd given himself over to another bout with pornography. I encouraged him to describe to me what goes on in his heart in the hours following another fall.

He began to describe the levels of anguish and disgust that would roll over his spirit. He told me how dirty and shameful he felt inside because of what he'd done. He'd go into a state of mourning over who he felt himself becoming, and the thought of what he'd just done was almost enough to make him vomit.

As he continued sharing his feelings, I interrupted him with a simple statement. I told him that when God looks at him, He sees his heart, and God is delighted at what He sees. I told him he had God's heart and he didn't even know it. He despised the same things God despises. And he was sickened by the very things God is sickened by. The fact that this precious man felt the way he did about his sins was evidence that he had God's heart. The truth about this man was not the things he struggled with; the truth about him was in his heart. This is the truth that God sees.

The bondage this man was under was not the pornography; it was the names he began calling himself because of the pornography. When he realized how his Father in heaven saw him, he began to see himself in that same light, and the moment he did, he walked away from the pornography. It's imperative to understand that God rejoices in the truth about you. Therein lies the secret to freedom from every sin with which you struggle. It's the truth that sets us free.

God is not bound by time and space. He knows our future as well as our present. When He looks at us, He calls us by what He sees in our future, not by what we see now. With God, the future is as solid and real as the present is to us. When He looks at us, it's important to know that He is not "hopeful" for what we could become, but of who we are in the "eternal future," what we *will* become and already are to Him outside of time. This is the truth that God rejoices in, and this is the name by which He calls us.

God saw the future of a man named Abram, and He gave him the name Abraham. God said He would make this childless man "the father of many nations." Then He went on to say, "It has been done." God didn't say it would happen in the future. To Him, it was the truth in the present and He called him by that name.

God approached a cowardly man hiding in a cave and called him a "mighty warrior." Gideon's reaction was the same as ours would have been. He began to correct God with a long list of things by which he defined himself as anything but a warrior. But God interrupted him and told him the truth. He was a mighty warrior whether it had come to pass yet or not. It was the truth, a truth that God rejoiced in.

When God looks at you, He calls you by a name that has nothing to do with your present situation or mind-set. Be excited about that! And stop calling yourself the lying names of your present. There is a truth about you that is so wonderful and enticing that God can't contain Himself when He looks at you. He sees that and only that.

God is pleased to reveal Himself to the world in the most common and easily understood way. He rejoices in the fact that everyone can connect and relate to Him. God has made the truth so basic and simple that even little children can know Him personally. God rejoices in the bare facts about us and the simplicity of who Christ is. Love rejoices in truth, unvarnished and ever so uncomplicated.

God also rejoices in the truth about spirituality. Jesus once looked up to heaven and said, "Thank You, Father, for keeping this hidden from the wise and learned and revealing it to the little children." As I said in chapter 1, anytime someone gives you a new deep and profound spiritual truth about God's heart that you didn't already know in your own heart, you can pretty much count on its not being true. The truth is not some deep well of knowledge that only the educated professors can unlock. It doesn't take four years of Bible college and a knowledge of Greek and Hebrew. The truth is already in you. It's in little children. When you hear it, it should be something that you already knew in your heart to be true. With Jesus Christ, what you see is what you get. Either you accept it or you reject it. Jesus is the mystery revealed. He is not a mystery that is still being revealed. He plainly said that if we love, we will know God; if we don't love, we won't know God. Don't look any deeper. People who truly love never question the truth of this. Only those who don't love reject this truth, probing the Scriptures for something more filling for their spiritual bellies.

Keep this in mind. All truth must pass the "child test." If a child intuitively understands it, it's probably truth. But if it's too complicated or doesn't match what a child inherently knows, it's probably a lie. If you want to know God's heart, you must learn to think simply and with your heart as a little child does. The harder you try to intellectualize faith, the further away you'll get from understanding.

The love in our hearts is what wins people to God. We don't have to embellish the truth to get people interested in Him. Love is the truth. This, and only this, is what God delights in. He delights in love because it's the most powerful force in the world. If we don't know this love, we're left to nothing but our own deceitfully coercive efforts to convince people to come to our churches.

When we understand that God rejoices in what He sees in us, we can be freed to believe our next subject as well.

CHAPTER 14

The Distant God?

B y the time I was seven, my teachers had discovered I
had a severe learning disability. Dyslexia had not yet
been named, so I didn't have the luxury of a cool medical
term. Back then, the term was "stupid." I couldn't read to
save my life.

By the time I reached high school, I was at a third-grade
reading level. In fact, I was at a third-grade level in every area.
Most of my reading at school was spent in "special reading,"
drawing pictures and writing short stories—basically what
they have you do when they don't know what else to do.

My five brothers and sisters all did exceptionally well in
school. So I felt singled out. Imagine my baby sister, seven
years younger, helping me sound out the words on my tenth-
grade homework assignment. I wondered why this was happening to me, and I asked that question hundreds, probably
thousands of times.

The biggest and perhaps most negative effect on my aca-
demic performance was my third-grade teacher. She was the
one who discovered I had a learning disability coupled with
extreme attention deficit disorder (which of course, there was
no term for then either). A harsh woman with a gruff voice,
she was extremely condescending. I recall looking in her eyes
at eight years of age and seeing clearly that she detested me.
Being hated by an adult was defining for me. It drained every

bit of confidence right out of me. I truly wanted to please her, but no matter what I did she humiliated me all the more.

I'd regularly find myself standing in front of the class, being asked questions she specifically knew I didn't have answers to for the purpose of humiliating me. She probably believed it would encourage me to try harder and apply myself, but I believe she got a secret thrill out of it, because even after I'd break down and cry, she'd simply stand there and watch. I've never been able to describe the horror of that period of my life, and to this day I have nightmares about it. It changed the course of my life for twenty years following.

Every morning as I set out for school, I was walking to a torture camp. As I left my neighborhood and walked through the Arizona desert, my legs became weak and my heart pounded in my chest. The moment my school came into view, I'd feel a lump in my throat and my eyes would burn with tears. Every morning I became a dead man walking to the gas chamber.

A metal bridge hung over the busy street in front of my school. Crossing that bridge every morning was crossing into hell. Every day I stood at the top of that ugly brown bridge and peered across, the dread churning in my gut. As I walked that final twenty yards across that bridge, I'd look over the side and watch the speeding cars race beneath. I wondered where they might be going in such a hurry. And I wished I could be in one of them instead of on that bridge.

As I reflect back on it today, I realize that every morning a transformation took place in my heart as I crossed the bridge. I became someone else. I had to in order to survive. When school was out and I was crossing that bridge on my way home, I could be me again. But the next morning, I'd depart from myself again before crossing back to school.

One day I sat down in the middle of that bridge, unable

to cross. I never went to school at all. I just sat there and thought. I dreamed that there was something wonderful just beyond that old bridge instead of my elementary school. I squinted to see the faces of the people driving beneath me. I even considered jumping off that bridge and ending it all. I sat there all day, just thinking. I thought about my father and where he might be. I imagined he was sitting on the bridge beside me holding my hand. I dreamed he'd walk across with me and sit with me in class to protect me and comfort me if things got bad. But when I opened my eyes, he wasn't there. So I just sat there some more.

As the years passed, I often wondered where God was during that time in my life. Why didn't He protect me? How could He just sit there and allow this woman to hurt me? Surely God was aware. Where was this protection I had heard so much about?

We all have something in our lives we wish we could have been protected from. But what we want isn't always what's best for us. In the name of protecting our kids, we sanitize our homes to keep harmful bacteria out, never thinking that children may need to develop the ability to fight off those bacteria to survive later in life. They need to get sick every now and then. Sometimes what we think of as protection could actually be a curse. We've come to define being protected as nothing bad ever happening to our flesh. As long as the flesh is protected, we think we're fine. But what about the spirit and the heart? What of the selfishness that breeds this upside-down view of protection?

The problem with our modern-day definition of protection is that it's shallow and nearsighted. We've actually *depersonalized* it and made it into a mindless concept that should fit every person in every situation. And this cookie-cutter view of protection also depersonalizes our relationship with God.

Eventually we begin to expect everything, including God, to work in a one-size-fits-all way, like a vending machine. This mind-set is not conducive to relationship. In fact, it's anti-relationship. Let me explain.

We've all heard stories of someone in a severe car accident who escaped without a scratch. Someone will say, "God protected him." And maybe He did. But when we define God's protection this way, we make a grave mistake. What about the thousands of loving people who haven't escaped accidents without a scratch? Was God not protecting them? If we define protection this way, we're forced to assume God protects some and not others. This is how people in the church I was raised in believed, and it's how many people see God today.

These robotic expectations of protection have woven themselves into every area of our religious thinking. His ways eventually become a mystery to us because they don't coincide with our idea of this universal law. God becomes like an irritating soda machine that has a mind of its own. It's not supposed to work this way, but for some mysterious reason it does. This is why so many people behave as they do when the soda doesn't come down the chute. They get angry and start slamming the machine with their fists. This isn't supposed to happen. They followed all the rules. They put the exact amount in the slot. They pushed all the right buttons. Yet they didn't get what they were "promised."

If you ask people if they believe that God always protects, they may say, "Yes. Of course." But most Christians agree that God *doesn't always* protect. Those who believe He does usually believe His protection is contingent on our toeing the line and earning it. So we say things like, "If that person doesn't turn from what they're doing, God will 'lift His hand of protection' from them." This is how we explain tragedy in other people's lives. We think He does this because our mechanical definition of protection tells us that's what it is.

I've heard God's protection described as an umbrella, and if we step out from underneath it, we'll get rained on. We have a one-dimensional understanding of God's protection that is contingent on our following an impossible list of laws and guidelines in an effort to earn it. At any point when something bad happens, we can always find a rule on that list we overlooked and blame ourselves for stepping outside His protection. I became an expert at finding these things in my life. I could find a reason to blame myself for every bad thing that happened to me.

I know people who can't drive their cars to the grocery store without asking God to place angels around them for "protection." The heart of that kind of prayer is fear that we don't already have that protection. We fear it because we've been taught that nothing is free, and love does not always protect us unless we somehow pay for it.

Thousands of well-meaning Christians offer up daily prayers to "Father God" for His hand of protection over their families, businesses, and homes. They approach Him with fear. "Father God, I've paid my tithe this month, so please protect my business." "Father God, hold back the demons from attacking my family." "Father God, please put angels around my home to guard it and protect it." What they really mean is, "Godfather, remember me."

Modern Christians teach that we're to pay tithes to God, like buying protection from a mafia kingpin who first requires our loyal payment. This is the picture we've painted of our Father in the twenty-first century, and it's repulsive and heartbreaking. I don't know if there is another teaching that's so far removed from love. And yet amazingly, like marching droids, we accept it as fact and write the check in fear, hoping God will do what the preacher promised.

How difficult is it to believe that God will always protect you when you've grown up with the wrath of God hanging over your head at every turn? When I was a kid, I was more worried about finding someone to protect me from God than I was about getting God to protect me. It seemed every other sermon made mention of His wrath in some way. He was the last person I'd run to if I was in trouble. If anything, I'd run the other way.

If I wasn't going to be destroyed by His wrath, one of His tough lessons where He sends unbelievable hardship in life would eventually do me in. Expecting protection from Him became a ridiculous notion, especially when everything I had been taught suggested He was the one causing the bad things to happen in the first place. Most of my Christian friends felt the same way. I believe that with today's understanding of God's heart, it is next to impossible to believe that love always protects.

God Always Protects

God protects you because He loves you. Not because you are being good and following the rules. Protection is a sacred thing with love. It's never used to manipulate or control. He would never threaten to take it away for the purpose of getting your attention. Just as we would never think of using this against our children, God won't do it with you. There are plenty of loving ways to get someone's attention without using fear.

Know for sure that God will never, ever lift His hand of

protection from you! Your security is sacred to Him. Without it, you are nothing and He knows that. We live in a world where things go wrong. Bad things happen to all people eventually. It's just a fact of life. Don't ever suspect that God has removed His protection in an effort to correct, rebuke, or punish you when something bad happens in your life. He never once promised us that nothing bad would ever happen to us. As long as you are here on earth, you will experience adversity and pain. Everyone does. You must know in your heart that when you do, it's not a sign that God has ceased to protect you, and it certainly is not God bringing on the bad thing in order to teach you a lesson. At times, you might allow your children to experience hardship to teach them a lesson they'll need later in life. But intentionally hurting your child? Love never thinks this way.

God's protection is a Father's promise to always hold us up in the midst of all circumstances no matter how terrible. Love bears up under anything! It is the support beam that will never give way, even in the midst of unimaginable pressure. The pressures and pains of life are not evidence of a lack of protection; they are the things that prove God's protection.

Understand that there is no escape from adversity and hardship as long as we live in this world. Bad things happen not only to bad people but to all people. The good news is, God will never cease to support and grow our hearts regardless of what is thrown at the flesh. God will never override the heart to save the flesh. Everything He does is for the heart because that's the part of you that lasts forever. Love always thinks this way. It's all about the heart.

God is a heart person, and we are created in His image. Though the flesh and the heart are interwoven, it's imperative that all things of God are seen and understood through the lens of the heart and not the flesh. The flesh is temporary, but the heart is eternal. This is why teachers who say we cannot trust our hearts are so paralyzing.

When we think of the modern link between paying tithes and God's protection, it's interesting to note that none of the New Testament writers talked about paying tithes. Why would that be? Maybe it's because the New Testament is all about relationship. And if you love, giving only 10 percent is ridiculous and offensive because love gives *everything*.

I'm not suggesting God has changed from Old Testament times. God never changed, nor will He ever change; but *circumstances* have changed. When I married my beautiful wife, one day earlier, there were limitations to our relationship that prohibited us from experiencing intimacy. Twenty-four hours later, those boundaries were removed. We hadn't changed; *circumstances* did.

Until we understand what has changed because of Christ, we will always be bound to the unmarried mentality of the Old Testament. In many ways the church resembles a couple who have dated for fifty years and never entered into marriage. This is what our teachings do today. They reject the intimacy that Christ died for and embrace an anti-relationship mentality of solitude. In Old Testament times, people paid. In New Testament times, we give. The difference between the two is the revelation of love. You don't have to pay God for His protection. God always protects you, and His protection is free because He's married to you.

The wrath of God should never scare you. All human beings have something in them that needs to know that their dad can beat up all other dads. It's a security issue. From the earliest ages on the playground, kids are disputing back and forth as to whose dad is invincible. The wrath of God is never pointed toward His children. It's used on *behalf* of His children. Sadly, however, we've been made to believe He would someday point His wrath toward His own children. Because of this, we suspect that every bad thing in our lives is God giving us what we deserve.

It was a difficult day for me when my oldest daughter had her first vaccination shots. Watching her go through the fear and pain of that brought my wife and me to tears. I remember her eyes when the first needle pierced her skin. I laid my body over hers and cried with her through the experience. The look on her face was one of total disillusionment. She seemed to be searching for why I would do this to her. She thought I was causing this pain. I couldn't explain that I did this because I love her. I did it to *protect* her from something that could hurt her far worse in the future. It didn't make it any easier, but it *had* to happen.

When we get a vaccination, we are actually being injected with the very thing we are trying to avoid. With a smallpox vaccination, the doctor is purposefully shooting smallpox into our bodies. The same is true with the measles, the mumps, and even the flu vaccine. Ironically, this is what it takes to be inoculated from these deadly diseases in the future.

Many people live bitter lives thinking the pain of their past was evidence that God wasn't there to protect them. They never stop to ask what it is they've been inoculated against because of those experiences. Rather than embrace who they are today as a result of those vaccinations of the past, they choose to focus on the pain of the shot.

People who grow up in a stressful home where tension is always looming are inoculated against being unable to face tense situations later in life. They become uniquely qualified because of it. Emotional vaccinations often uniquely fit our futures. With God, our protection has to do with our purpose. When He created you, He knew your purpose and what kind of vaccinations you'd need to shape you. God did not delight in that torment you may have endured, nor did He cause it. He did not even plan for it to happen. In the midst of it happening, however, He used it to strengthen your ultimate purpose in life.

But He was there with you, crying and holding your hand, just as I was the day my daughter Landin received her shots. It's worth it to Him because He knows that the pain you are being injected with has everything to do with your purpose. That's where He knows you'll find your maximum level of happiness and satisfaction. That's the thing about a purpose: it's custom-made for *you*. It was specifically fitted to your personality. Unfortunately, if we are not careful, we can end up focusing our entire lives on the things that happened to us and how awful they were to endure. When we go down this road, we are the ones rejecting our purpose, and until we decide to embrace who we have become as a result of our past, our purpose will go unfulfilled.

Ten years ago I arrived in Phoenix, Arizona, from Hollywood, California, to attend a ministry training program. It was like an evangelism boot-camp of training for people in outreach and youth ministries. I had sold everything I owned and moved to Phoenix to attend this nationwide program in hopes that it would be my entrance into the ministry.

The day it began, I was driving to the church on a road I'd never been on before. I was excited, anticipating what the coming weeks and months would hold. And as I was praying and thinking about everything I'd been through in the last thirty years up to then, I casually looked up from the road, and *there was the ugly brown bridge.*

I almost stopped breathing when I saw it. It wasn't supposed to be there. But I'd know that thing anywhere from a hundred yards. Nevertheless, almost twenty miles away from the place it had been where I grew up, there stood the metal bridge I used to cross every day to school. Evidently the city had moved it to this little street I was driving down. I later learned it was considered one of the biggest recycling projects in Arizona.

And as I passed beneath the bridge on my way to church, I looked up and there, as God is my witness, a little boy was looking over the side at me. And without any warning, I began to cry. I sobbed for the boy I'd been as my mind flooded with the memories of that terrible bridge, those terrible walks, and all the hours I'd spent in misery on its metal tresses as a child. In that moment, the Lord spoke to me about my purpose in life.

He began to reveal that everything I went through as a child was preparing me for my purpose in life. He said knowing I was being prepared didn't make allowing me to experience those things any easier for Him, but they had to happen. I was meant to listen and uniquely understand hurting people. I was meant to love those who felt abandoned and encourage those with low confidence. And I truly *do* love them. My heart bleeds for them. I can't help myself; it's just a part of me. Every grueling experience I endured as a child was heart preparation that would allow me to bring maximum joy and contentment to my life and others' lives.

I realized then that the real me is intricately woven together with my purpose in life. I learned that most people have separated the two and see protection only as it pertains to their flesh. Even the things that happened to me in an attempt to destroy my purpose were later used to build it up. God's protection is much deeper than I had ever realized.

Looking back on the pain of my past in the light of what I'm doing now, I wouldn't change a single thing. He was protecting me all along. It was worth it, and I would do it all again.

It was He who held me up when my teacher humiliated me in front of the class. It was He who walked me across the bridge to school when I was eight years old and terrified. He was even there the day I sat on that bridge and contemplated jumping off. He was holding me up in the midst of pressure and torment, and He has never failed me yet. Love always protects.

CHAPTER 15

The Untrustworthy God?

My house looks like a day-care center. With four daughters and a young son, from morning to night there is noise: sounds of giggling, whining, crying, playing, and laughter. There is rarely a moment of quiet. But believe it or not, I actually look forward to coming home to the chaos of the screaming five. It's where I belong, and I wouldn't give it up for the world.

And every so often, I am reminded of the power of my responsibility as their father. It's a thousand times more than providing food and shelter. That's about 3 percent of my job. My true purpose springs to life the moment I look into their eyes and I see their unconditional, wholehearted trust in me. Seeing that is almost more than I can bear.

If they knew the truth about my humanity, I suspect they would feel less confidence in Daddy. Nevertheless, they fall asleep in my arms in a public place without even a hint of worry. They leap off the edge of the pool into my arms without reservation. They beg me to play "blast off" and throw them up high into the air and catch them while their mother nervously watches. The sun rises and sets at my command, as far as they're concerned. No other man is better-looking, stronger, or smarter than me. My words determine the course of their lives. My eyes reveal who they are, and my kisses bring healing to their "owies."

It is difficult for me to imagine that someday their trust might wither away from me. The thought of that happening makes me ill. If that gaze of belief in their eyes were to leave, I'm not sure I'd fully know who *I* was anymore. Within that look lies the power that drives me to great exploits on their behalf. It kills every selfish part of me and purifies my heart.

And though the complete trust of a child is not rare, few people in today's world believe in their hearts that love always trusts. While the majority would unanimously agree that it should trust, they would tell you the reality is that it simply doesn't.

Our understanding of the concept of trust has taken a serious beating in this generation. We define it according to how it pertains to us in the here and now. We want to know if we can trust someone to be faithful to us or to tell us the truth. We question whether or not a person can be trusted to keep our secrets or to not talk badly about us behind our back. If someone proves themselves *worthy* of our trust, then we say we'll trust them—conditionally.

In today's thinking, all people start with a zero balance of trust. Whatever they get from that point on is *earned*. If they mess up, they're catapulted back to zero and made to start over. Some people are more extreme with their trust rules than others. And some have simply stopped trusting anyone.

A lack of trust has become a sign of strength in today's society. All the heroes in our favorite action movies have renounced trust altogether. It's seen as not only independent and powerful, but also "streetwise." It's the greatest form of self-protection we know. Many people, even Christians, build walls around their hearts so that no one gets in and no one gets out.

Like the term "protection," the true significance of the word *trust* has become shallow and superficial. And as long as trust is seen from this selfish, upside-down perspective, we'll never understand its true beauty or possess its power. We will also ultimately define God's heart and our relationship with Him accordingly.

The evidence of this shallow view of trust is everywhere in the church today. Often, Christians believe God would have them consider everyone trustworthy—because this is the extreme opposite of the world's view. This misguided notion has proven a huge problem for thousands of well-intentioned people, making them easy targets for deception. I've watched women stay with abusive or alcoholic boyfriends who are cheating on them simply because they think trusting them is the Christian thing to do. Con artists have learned to play the God card when approaching people who go to church. Say "God bless," and you're likely to get the Christian handout. While not every Christian is this naive, there are many who honestly believe they are supposed to be. It is not uncommon for us to point our fingers at someone who refuses us something and say, "I thought you were a Christian!"

After being personally ripped off many times because of my misguided concept of trust, I became fearful of a trusting God. If God was love and love always trusted, then I wasn't sure if I could trust God. He might release Charles Manson from prison or call an ex–child molester to work in my child's day care. The thought of God being so trusting frightened me to death. The biggest problem with our mixed-up view of trust is that it makes trusting God a terrifying prospect.

We actually fear that He might send us to a foreign country to be a missionary or call us to marry someone we don't want. We've been taught not to link trust with heart knowledge. Many of us believe that God doesn't take into account who we are or what we prefer. He just commands us to do stuff, and we are required to trust Him and obey.

Trusting God was presented to many of us as an order. It was something we were required to do if we wanted to be rewarded with anything good. Whether or not it flowed from anything real and authentic wasn't the issue. Putting trust in God was a measurement of faith. If I found myself worrying or doubting anything in life, it was as good as telling Him I didn't love Him. The condemnation I went through each time I worried or felt abandoned was more than I could bear. I wasn't allowed to have those feelings.

The God I was raised with was like a controlling, abusive husband with an insecurity complex. He wanted my trust so He would feel powerful. I couldn't so much as question anything without making Him furious. Coming to trust God was never presented to me as something that evolved naturally out of love. It was an obligation that you did out of fear, not love.

I grew up hearing the preacher tell us that God wouldn't bless us until He could first trust us. I quickly learned that I shouldn't expect any real blessing from Him because I had proven a thousand times over that I'd screw it all up in the end. So I quit asking. Then I went down the same road I've seen hundreds of others travel since. I began performing for Him in an effort to convince Him I was good and wouldn't drop the ball. I attended church faithfully and gave in the offering. This was how I would prove myself to God. But something inside me knew that He would never trust me because He and I both knew I wasn't worthy of it. He knew the inner me and so did I. I had a long way to go before the inner me would be worthy of trust.

I was taught that God would do nothing but put me through test after test in life. Everything was a test. He was constantly testing me to see if I was trustworthy. It was exhausting and irritating because it seemed I never knew

I was being tested until I had already failed. Every time I stopped and graded myself, I found I'd failed once again. I was like most well-meaning Christians; I didn't believe for one minute that God always trusted. I believed He never trusted and always tested. If we believe He trusts us, why would we think He'd keep testing us all the time? This mentality comes from our worldly perspective of trust. We think it must be earned first. Only if someone passes the test are they finally trustworthy.

Many of us can't fathom God as having an open heart because of the many times we have been blackballed by fellow Christians in the past for something we did or did not do. The moment we step out of line, we find that "godly" people who were once our friends suddenly refuse to have anything to do with us. It's difficult not to make assumptions about the heart of God from the actions of His children. And we all are ultimately conformed to the image of who we believe our Father in heaven is. Christians close their heart doors to people who anger them because that's who they believe their Father is.

I believe that the entire concept of "backsliding" is built on an inner belief that God closes His heart off to us when we make mistakes. A person sins, and they immediately feel that God has turned His heart from them. They decide to wait a few days before approaching God, and in the midst of those few days, they sin again. Now they are forced to wait an additional few days, and almost always they sin once more in that time. Before they know it, they have assumed a life emotionally separate from God for several years because they believed in their heart that God turned His back on them when they sinned.

When we feel we can't approach God with confidence and boldness, we're declaring that we don't believe God always trusts. When we find ourselves performing for God in order to prove our trustworthiness, we're showing that we believe we have to earn His trust. When we feel extra bold and secure in His presence because we've been really good in the past week or two, we are subtly admitting that we don't believe His heart is always open to us. Anytime we feel closer and more accepted by Him because we followed the rules, we're showing our belief that God does not always trust.

Here's the problem: our view of trust has to do with acts, external proof, and being or becoming worthy. We focus on the things we want from God, and if we get them, we trust Him. If we don't; we won't. And we believe He acts this way too. If He gets the behavior He wants from us, He'll trust us. Because our eyes are on the physical things we want and not on the true desires of our hearts, we determine His trustworthiness by whether or not we get the promotion at work or the car we prayed for. If our car breaks down or we get an unexpected bill in the mail, then God's trustworthiness is in question.

Why do we believe God acts this way? Why would His trust be conditional? Doesn't He really always trust in us and believe in us? While the answer from our mouths might be an easy yes, I wonder what answer our hearts would give. I have found that with all the religious jargon in the world today, it is next to impossible to believe that God's heart is always open to us, whatever our situation in life.

God Always Trusts

We all have within us the need to know that we are trusted by our Father. We define ourselves and our worthiness by how open we feel His heart is to us. If we perceive it to be closed, we will spiritually and emotionally die. The label "unworthy" will follow us wherever we go. This is devastating to the human heart, because whatever our Creator believes about us is what we will ultimately become. His trust is the thing that holds us together, lifts us up, and propels us forward.

I've found that when I tell most Christians that God believes in them, they tend to be unaffected by that statement because of the watered-down theology they've adopted. They'll say, "I know He believes in me," but I can immediately tell what they're really saying. They're really saying, "God believes in my potential and what I could become, but as I am here and now—He doesn't believe in that." Nothing could be further from the truth. Though God clearly sees what you will become in the future, believe it or not, He also loves who you are today.

We see trust from an outward perspective. We think it pertains to things and topics and instances. God sees trust as it pertains to the heart. We ask, What does trust look like on the outside and how are we affected in the physical realm? God asks what it looks like on the inside and what the spiritual effects are. What does the heart look like when it is trusting? What is its position and attitude? If we can define that, we will have discovered the true meaning of trust.

The unfortunate thing about the way we measure trust is that it can be counterfeited. We can act like we trust someone when the real posture of our hearts is positioned to the contrary. Even worse, some people can get us to position our hearts to trust by imitating actions we hold as evidence of trustworthiness, when in reality they are actually pulling one over on us. This is particularly devastating because the person's heart position is being governed by evidence rather than love. It almost always ends in heartbreak.

Evidence will always fail, turn, or change. Love is

unchanging. This is why so many of us have become heart-broken. We've positioned our hearts in a trust stance based on outward evidence. When the evidence turned, our hearts broke. If we had taken a trust stance out of love, no turning, failing, or changing could ever break our hearts.

What the world fails to see is that trust is not about whether you get what you want or are allowed to do this or that. It's not about the outward manifestations of the flesh by which we have defined it. Though I don't hand my five-year-old daughter the keys to my car and tell her to take it for a spin, that doesn't mean I don't trust her, love her, or cherish her. In fact, if anything, it shows that I do trust her (love her, respect her, know her) beyond her ability to drive a car. She doesn't know how to drive. Her feet wouldn't reach the gas pedal. My decision not to give her the keys has nothing to do with my deeper trust in my daughter, and everything to do with my love for her. Trusting my daughter is far deeper than giving her permission to risk her life. If she makes driving the car a trust issue, she'd be missing the essence of trust. Trust is a heart condition, not a physical action.

There is a difference between God's trust and His wisdom. We commonly confuse the two and end up thinking God doesn't trust us. It is possible to deny an ex–child molester a position in a day-care facility and keep our heart doors open to them at the same time. It is possible to not allow someone to abuse us and still keep our hearts opened to them. Just because we may not give a man who has a gambling problem the position of accountant and treasurer doesn't mean we have to close our hearts to him.

God's trust cannot be summed up by the things He does or doesn't give us. Giving us what we think is best for us isn't a matter of trust; it's a matter of God's deeper wisdom. Many people pray for God to send them a mate, but it may not be the right time. God's wisdom does not allow Him to toss that person the keys to a relationship they're incapable of driving at this point in their life. It's not about trust; it's about wisdom. God can do this and keep His heart fully open to that person at the same time.

One of the things I've found about God's heart is that He hears our hearts over our mouths. We are in the habit of asking Him for things that are contrary to what our hearts desire. Most people are not even in touch with their own hearts, so when God answers the prayers of their hearts over the prayers of their mouths, they are mystified and perplexed. Their entire lives have been full of answered prayers, but they don't know it because they never heard themselves ask for what they received in the first place. Because they didn't get the *things* that their mouths asked for here and now, they stopped trusting God from their hearts.

I know men who have completely closed their hearts off from women. They don't trust them as far as they could throw them. I know women who feel this way about men. Their hearts are so miserably untrusting and clogged because of the pain of their past that they are actually fearful of the idea of opening up to a member of the opposite sex. Ironically, men and women who feel this way almost always pray (with their mouths) and ask God to send them a mate. When it doesn't happen, they lose all trust in God because it appears that He did not answer their prayers. The problem is that God did respond to their prayers, they just don't remember praying for what they received. God is a heart person. He listens and speaks only to the heart. Our answers from God are in accordance with our hearts' prayers, not our mouths'.

One of the learning channels that my wife and I watch regularly had a special on emergency room traumas. We usually don't allow gory shows into our home, but this was an educational channel, so it kind of made it legal gore. One of the first patients to arrive in the emergency room was a man who had been shot in the chest. There were about six doctors around him working feverishly to save his life. At one point he "flatlined" and they brought out the shockers to bring him back to life. When that didn't work, they decided to massage his heart manually. To do this, they brought out a big saw and literally cut right through his sternum. They made doors in his chest so they could get to his heart. Once this poor man was opened up, the doctor reached inside him and massaged his heart until the man had a pulse again. It was the most astounding thing I had ever witnessed.

In the midst of watching this play out in my living room, God began to show me that this is what He requires in a true relationship. Total openness! Complete vulnerability! For any relationship to be authentic, the heart doors of both people must always be open. The trust we're talking about here is essentially a position of the heart that creates an environment of total openness and vulnerability. It's the environment in which true, pure love can exist.

Imagine the level of trust this man would have had to have if his eyes opened in the midst of this procedure. Every hidden part of him was exposed for the purpose of saving his life. If he had refused access to his heart, he certainly would have died. Real relationships are the same way. If the heart doors are not open, the relationship will wither and eventually die. This principle runs throughout many aspects of love. It is a beautiful picture of who God is when He comes to you.

It's important to God that we know He trusts, that even when we aren't particularly trustworthy, His heart doors are still wide open to us. It's essential that we trust He will apply His wisdom to our lives at any cost and never close His heart to us. This is possible only if we understand the difference between the manifestations of trust on the inside and our preconceived expectations of trust on the outside.

The last scene of Jesus' life was every bit as gory as that show I watched that day. He was exposed and opened up before us. God introducing Himself to the world was a perfect picture of how He expresses Himself in the context of relationship. He keeps nothing hidden from His children. Everything has been exposed for you to see because that is what relationship requires. Don't ever think that God will stop trusting in you if you mess up. Your actions have no bearing on His perfect trust in you. He is the author of trust and openness. Rest in that and rejoice, because your Father in heaven loves you, and love always trusts!

CHAPTER 16

The Disappointed God?

It didn't matter on this day if the other kids made fun of me or picked me last for their team. It didn't matter if I couldn't read or write as well as the other children, or if I sat alone in the lunchroom. It didn't even matter if the teacher humiliated me in front of the class. Today, it just didn't matter because I was holding something no one else had. It got me through the day. It made awful things trivial and sad things happy. This day was different from any other day because this was the day my parents showed me the tickets to Disneyland that they had bought the day before. We were going in three months, and nothing else between now and then could matter nearly as much.

When life got hard, I'd just remind myself I was going to Disneyland in three months, and I'd be happy for another day. When worry overtook me the night before school, I would remind myself that I was going to Disneyland in three months and worry left me alone. I had been given a hope to anchor myself to. As long as the tickets were stuck to the refrigerator and the date was set on the family calendar, I was bigger than the normal me.

My mind would skip ahead, rehearsing the things I might do. I'd picture myself waiting in line for a ride with popcorn in one hand and a corn dog in the other. At night when everyone was sleeping, I would lie in bed and close my eyes, and if I tried really hard, I could almost hear the sounds and smell the popcorny air of the Magic Kingdom. I would get that feeling like when I used to lie under the Christmas tree and look up at the lights and ornaments, dreaming of Christmas Day. There is nothing like that feeling. Many nights it rocked me to sleep like a caring mother.

Most people think of hope as a dreamy fantasy that doesn't have much bearing on reality. We think of it as optimism in the midst of struggle or turmoil. A "hopeful" person might say, "It would be great if that happened," or "Oh, I hope this is true." Irrespective of their situation, they "hold out hope" by being positive.

Children *hope* they can be a ballerina or a professional baseball player. Women *hope* they don't gain weight, and men *hope* they make a lot of money. Terminally ill patients *hope* they beat the sickness. Prisoners *hope* they'll be released early, and everyone else *hopes* they won't.

Though most of these things are possible, they are not probable. However, our view of hope chooses to make them at least appear probable for the moment. It gives us what we need to get us through the day. If it doesn't happen, that's okay, too; at least we didn't give up *hope*.

The problem with this definition of hope is that it has been reduced to *wishing* for something. There's no certainty or guarantee. It's just a dream of what could possibly take place. There isn't anything wrong with wishing and dreaming, but when it takes the place of real hope, we are making a grave mistake. The inevitable end of that mind-set is hopelessness.

Every time I read about the "hope" we have in Christ, I would wonder what Paul meant. He would talk about how Jesus Christ had risen from the dead and was now at the right hand of the Father, interceding for us. Then out of the blue he would say he *hopes* this is true. *Which is it?* I would wonder. *Is it true or not?* It almost had a tone of uncertainty to it when I read it. How can you know something is true and then *hope* it's true in the same breath? It sounded to me as if Paul wasn't sure whether Christ rose from the dead or not.

If *God is love* and *love always hopes*, what does that mean? Why would God need to hope for anything if He already knows the beginning from the end? Does God block from His mind what He knows will happen so He can hope it will happen with us? That sounds a bit weird to me.

Similar to what we've done to the words *protect* and *trust*, our definition of *hope* has been twisted. And once again, the new revised version comes out looking like the exact opposite of the real thing. Each time we do this in the English language, we set ourselves up for unparalleled destruction. The danger in this is that we ultimately end up believing that God's hope in us is actually hopeless. Hope is extremely precious; life depends on hope and God made it that way. It is very dear to His heart because of the power it possesses for His children when placed in the right things.

The purpose of *hope* is for it to be inserted into truth. This is the most important element of hope that we must understand. Hope must always be inserted into truth. If it is placed in anything other than truth, it becomes a destructive force that can potentially lead us into a world of emptiness and anguish.

When hope is placed in truth, it tows us through life's trials. There is nothing a person cannot endure if their hope is placed in truth. It was created for truth and nothing but truth. There is a hitch on the back of truth that we can connect our hope to that pulls us through challenges and circumstances we couldn't otherwise make it through.

But God also gives us a choice. We must choose where

to hitch our hope rope. There are also hitches on the backs of many counterfeit truths that will tow us to spiritual and emotional death. Anytime we willingly choose to tie our hope to something other than truth, we will be dragged to our deaths. This is why our definition of hope has been so damaged today. Generations of people have tied their hope ropes to lies and uncertainty. Because of this trend, our definition of hope has become distorted. Many have lost hope altogether because its new meaning doesn't have the truth we need attached to it. And as a result, hope has become nice to have but not indispensable.

When we lose our hope, we lose our faith as well. This is why so many women will tell you that they have lost all faith in men. They hitched their *hope ropes* to deception because those lies made them feel good for the moment. All the while, they said to themselves, "I hope he changes." Instead of putting their hope in the truth about men, they chose to put it in a fantasy or an idea they had created in their hearts. When we tie hope to something we know in our hearts is a lie but we wish in our heads wasn't, we are gambling with the true hope God provides. The end result is always hopelessness.

A man dates a woman who is promiscuous before marriage and then hopes she will settle down once she has a ring on her finger. When she starts flirting with his friends and the marriage finally ends, his hopes are dashed. A woman marries a man who has cheated on his wife to be with her in the hope that he won't leave her as well. When it happens, her hope is crushed and she loses faith in men altogether. A man gives up his job because he met a guy whose cousin's boyfriend's mother's aunt has an uncle who says he would hire him in a heartbeat. Before he knows it, he is living on the street and without hope.

What's worse is that many well-meaning people call

these desperate decisions "acts of faith." They think it's what God would have them do, to place their hope in false ideas regardless of the truth that surrounds them. Christians see godliness this way because this is how many people see God. They think God's heart asks them to blindly hope for anything they want as long as they "believe" in it strongly enough. The act of "hoping against all odds" feels spiritual to them because they've associated that with having faith. This grieves God because it assumes that He desires His children to build their homes on sinking sand. Hope was never meant for what could be or what might be. It was meant for what is, what was, and what will be.

Before we know it, we begin to hear God encouraging us to hope for the craziest things in the name of "faith." After so much trial and error, hope becomes almost impossible to sustain because its altered meaning has bitten us so many times. The unfortunate result is that we don't even hope in God anymore. His very existence begins to look like our definition of hope. Maybe He is real and maybe He isn't. Maybe He loves me and maybe He doesn't. He just might come through for me, but then again, He just might not. It's nice to think He will, but one can never be sure.

Hope that's attached to truth is vital because it's designed for the long haul. It's the assurance of the prize at the end of the race. Faith is what causes you to take each step along the way. Our hope must be in the truth at the end of the race. That truth is what makes the race worth running. If that truth is in question and our hope is not sure, it becomes merely a wish or a dream, and there's no endurance to keep running when the road gets bumpy and steep. The thing hope is placed in must be for sure if hope is going to receive its power when it's plugged in.

As a young pastor who fell head over heels in love with

people, I soon found that it's impossible to love people and purposefully cause them to question whether or not they will make it to heaven when they die. When we do this we are tampering with the most precious thing God has set before them. We are calling the prize at the end of the race into question, and we are covering it with doubt and uncertainty. The ultimate result is that the runner's hope is lost and the power to keep going is depleted. Love can't stomach the thought of dishing out uncertainty to people it adores. Hope was defined for me the day I fell in love with the people.

In the Christian world today, people have attached their hope to lies and been dragged to the point of becoming unrecognizable as Christians. It's an awful thought, but I fear it is not far from the truth. This happens because we are given mountains of theological and doctrinal points we are supposed to put our hope in. Before we know it we are going in a thousand different directions and arriving at nothing.

People who don't have hope in God must resort to substitutes to motivate them through trials in their lives. Pain and fear are common replacements. Imagine having fear of death as your only source of empowerment. Sadly, this is the case for many people. I've seen people become defensive the moment I attempt to cut the line they've attached to fear and offer them truth. They honestly feel they need that line to get to heaven. Cutting it is unthinkable. What would be there to motivate them to do right if it wasn't fear of not going? Ironically, this "hope in fear" has become a comfort over time.

God Always Hopes

When I was an eight-year-old boy, the hope that got me through the terrible times in my life was a few Disneyland tickets. Every time I came home after a hard day at school, I could look up and see those tickets on our refrigerator. I was going to Disneyland in three months. I needed that hope in order to make it through each day. If my parents had begun to threaten to tear up those tickets if I did something wrong, I would have lost my hope.

Imagine what happens when God's children believe they might not get to go to heaven if they make a mistake. Love could never threaten to tear up those tickets. God knows you need those tickets. The power of you knowing that those tickets are yours, and no one can take them from you, is the same power you need to get through life. Heaven is guaranteed to you because you need that guarantee. If you are a Christian and you don't believe you are secure in Christ, you have no hope. All you have is a wish and a dream. Until you know for sure that you belong to God and you are going to be with Him when you die, you will remain in a state of constant hopelessness. Everything in your life will waver, including your faith. This is precisely why so many Christians come and go from their faith all the time. They don't know for sure that they are okay with God. It all depends on their works and actions rather than what He promised.

The reason God has hope in you isn't because you've earned it. God knows the truth about you. And hope is always placed in truth. God's hope for you has to do with the truth that He has seen with His own eyes. When God looks at you today, He sees you in the future, and He calls you by that name. God is not trying to encourage you into who you could be or might be. He has seen your future and knows for a fact who you will become. His hope in you is placed in the truth of who you are becoming today, the future you.

He doesn't hope you will turn out better than you are now. He knows the outcome because He has seen it. He isn't unsure of the ending. He hopes in you because of His certainty of it. This is how He hopes you will hope. That's what true hope is: seeing the full truth and hoping in the assurance that truth will prevail in the end. This is why love always hopes, because love rejoices with the truth. The two go hand in hand. You can't have one without the other.

It is vital that you know your Father hopes in you because it speaks of your worth. When we think that God has lost hope in us, we begin to believe that He doesn't see any value in us. The truth is, He sees the future you and knows that it is worth every ounce of hope He has in you and for you. His hope in you is the evidence that your worth is far greater than you could ever imagine.

Not only do we need hope to survive, we need to know that God hopes in us as well. The moment we lose sight of this, we cease to matter in our own eyes. Every child searches their father's eyes to find that hope and approval. We were not only created to have hope in our Father, but we were created to find hope in Him as well.

God cares so much for you and your need for hope that He even supplies more hope where yours has been wasted. Even to those who waste it away on lies, He supplies fresh hope because He knows that His children need it to survive. Even when we continually make bad choices, it is never His desire to see us hopeless. When our wasted hope in untrue things comes to an end, and we are empty inside and without hope, God is there, supplying a new dose of it, because He knows that without hope we will never get better. I have watched in amazement His faithfulness in supplying hope to a generation of people who compulsively gamble it away on things that are sure to fail. He cares more about our well-being than He does about receiving our attention.

Because hope is so essential, it must be fiercely guarded.

And there's only one way to do that: by committing to truth. The pure, undiluted truth about God, faith, life, and yourself must be vigilantly protected and nourished. When something is added or taken away from pure truth, one of the consequences is a loss of hope. This is why you must guard what you allow yourself to listen to and believe. Everything that sounds good or feels right must first be measured against the infallible ruler God gave us—love. If anything other than the full definition of true love is used to gauge the authenticity of truth, it will deceive you, and the end result will be a total loss of hope.

Each aspect of love is interdependent. Like a delicate ecosystem, it depends on everything within it to sustain itself. Even the smallest eliminations can cause the biggest disasters. Take away ants or crickets from the earth, and the far-reaching effects would be devastating. The truth of God's heart is very much like this. This is why we must repair the fearful things we've believed about love. If we imply that God might turn His face from one of His children for something, we are creating a chain reaction of tiny explosions that get worse and worse down the line of our theology. The far-reaching effects of a wrong view of love on our belief system are devastating.

To preserve the truth about God's heart, every ingredient of love must be present. The moment we are envious we become impatient and self-seeking. If we are proud we become easily angered and rude. If we are boastful, we cannot be kind and we refuse to rejoice with the truth. If we don't rejoice with the truth, we will eventually lose our hope. Love requires each aspect to be in perfect alignment.

When a religion overlooks or disregards one aspect of love, it ultimately ends up redefining the face of God Himself. Over time, He begins to appear despicable and unattractive to people. It is absolutely imperative that we commit to truth and reject the lies that have swirled around us for so long. The only way to do this is to look into our hearts and remember what it was like as a child when our love was so pure and untainted. Remember how simple and real love was before life seeped in and complicated it so much? Return to that first love and embrace it, trust it, protect it, and watch it carry you to places you never imagined.

CHAPTER 17

The Disinterested God?

When the *Titanic* set sail, it was considered unsinkable. It was made of iron and was bigger than any cruise liner around. Because of this incredible feat of engineering, everyone believed this boat would persevere through anything. Great care was taken to see that the best of everything was on board—including crystal chandeliers, expensive china, and silver flatware. It was truly a five-star experience for its lucky passengers.

When the *Titanic* struck an iceberg and sank to the bottom of the ocean, many people speculated about what went wrong. Some people believed the ship was cursed. But others wondered how an iceberg could sink a ship that was made of iron. Survivors claimed the ship broke in half just before disappearing under the icy waters. Scientists argued for decades that it was impossible. It wasn't until they finally found the sunken ship that answers began to surface.

I learned about this on the Discovery Channel. They showed pictures from the wreckage site proving that the *Titanic* was indeed in two pieces. Further evidence showed that the iron used on the *Titanic* had not been tested. Because of the fact that the ship builders were rushing to complete the project by a certain time, they had decided not to take that one little step of testing the quality and durability of the iron. This proved to be a fateful choice. Tests have proven conclusively that the iron used to build the *Titanic* was as brittle as a pane of glass. It was doomed for failure the day it set sail.

The reality of the *Titanic* is that it really wasn't a boat at all. It was faking it. There was no way to tell the difference as it left the harbor with people clapping and music playing because it seemed to have everything. Who would have thought that what looked like a boat, floated like a boat, and felt like a boat, would turn out to be a coffin?

We have covered many different aspects of love thus far, and they all have one thing in common. They all can be faked. It is possible to fake patience and kindness. Anyone can fake not being envious or boastful or proud. Selflessness can be acted out and anger can be easily hidden. People can pretend not to keep records of wrongs, and it doesn't take much to act as though we don't delight in evil. Protection, trust, and even hope can be forged to look like the real things as well.

There is one last thing that is the final step to discovering the authenticity of love. Until it has been added to everything else, love is really not love yet. It may look like it, float like it, and even feel like it, but it's only a mirage. Before love leaves the assembly line and is given the label of authenticity, it must be tested. This testing is essential not only to prove it is really love, but also to survive, thrive, and grow. Love is useless and dormant, without purpose or function, unless it is tested. Before a professor is called a professor, he must first pass the tests that prove he is a professor. Though he may have all the knowledge inside, it amounts to nothing until he passes the test. A soldier is not a soldier until he has been proved in the heat of battle. He may look like a soldier and carry a gun. But until he passes the test under fire, he is just a guy playing soldier.

Perseverance is the result of combining all these essential qualities of true love. There is only one way to know for certain whether love is real or not. It has to make it through the fire. This is the one and only element of love that cannot be faked. Either it will persevere or it will melt away.

Today, we build our relationships the same way the *Titanic* was built. Testing a relationship before we go forward is the last thing on our minds. We minimize the need for perseverance in relationships today because we don't really want the truth. Often, we're looking for the quickest solution to our problem of pain or loneliness. As long as a relationship makes us feel good here and now, we aren't much concerned with whether or not it will persevere.

In my estimation, the majority of Christians have unequivocally failed this final test when it comes to their relationships with people in general. Countless times people have told me that when a disagreement or a problem arose in their churches, the Christians around them deserted them. I think the world in general would give us a failing grade in this area. Sadly, this has become the lens through which the world views God's heart. The bottom line is that though people say they know He is patient, kind, protective, trusting, and all those other things, when push comes to shove, they don't believe a word of it.

Couples who divorce don't often say their marriage "failed the test." Instead, they say, "We just grew apart," "We're just going in different directions," or "We just weren't meant to be together." Christians often say, "I don't think this was the person God had in mind for me," when their love couldn't take the heat of adversity. This is why people who have been married a long time know that the answer to whether or not it was love is found in whether or not the couple stuck it out. Are you still with that person? If not, love failed the test.

It may have looked and felt like love, but it wasn't. It was proven by the fire.

Many times we carry the belief that true love should never be tested at all. If trials come, we think that must mean the love isn't true. Testing it would be a lack of faith and would diminish its beauty.

I hear this a lot, and I get nervous when a couple sit in my office only weeks before their wedding date and tell me that they've never fought. Many of them think adversity hasn't come their way because their love is so real and strong. What a grave mistake. Compatibility is vital. But one of two things is often happening in relationships like this. First, the couple are likely avoiding conflict. And second, they're probably not talking about the things that really matter deeply to them. In the end, real love doesn't run from the testing; it embraces it.

Perhaps the most amazing evolution in our thinking on this is the fact that many people have come to believe that true love is supposed to fail the test. It's supposed to abandon you when you're most in need. We come up with clever terms that spin the meaning of love and excuse a failing grade. The term "tough love," which tries to use love as a behavior-modification tool, has made harsh treatment, emotional abuse, and even abandonment look biblical and wise. And there are times when love does require stepping back from the person who's abusing himself, others, or us. But the corruption of this concept ultimately has taught us to expect a failing grade, and when we get it, we somehow see that as evidence of true love. In short, we blame the heart.

We must have opposition and adversity to experience the incredible endurance, the perseverance of love. And yet, adversity is the very thing many people take as evidence of false love. We've learned that love is supposed to make suffering and hardship go away, but the truth is that nothing does that. The very purpose of love is to persevere and hold on in the midst of trials.

When I was in high school, I used to lift weights religiously (I repented of that years ago). But I discovered that there are two kinds of weight lifters in the world. There are the guys who lift for power and muscle, and there are the guys who lift for endurance. The endurance guys are usually lean and wiry. I've always thought they were just making excuses for their skinniness, but I have come to learn the importance of what they are doing. They put themselves under a continuous state of opposition in an effort to develop a strength that will carry them in the long run of life. The bulky guys, who lift for power and muscles, are seeking brute strength and a nice body. In the end, endurance wins out. Our world, however, has turned love into a picture of bulked-up attractive power and has downplayed and minimized love's need for endurance.

Some power-focused Christians teach that truly spiritual people never experience adversity, discouragement, or opposition. God will make the true spiritual giants rise above any trials they face in life. If someone is facing adversity, they must be doing something wrong. Unfortunately, this is simply not true. When the fire comes, the power seekers have no endurance because they have spent all their time praying away their trials. They pray for God to "bind all the demons" so that nothing will oppose them, and they escape adversity at every turn. The problem is, they become weak and frail in their hearts, and they don't last in the long run of life. When an iceberg comes their way, they break in half and sink to the bottom.

Many of us have been taught that all adversity is the result of sin or the devil. Before the fall of humankind, there was no adversity of any kind. But how can that be? Adversity is actually a beautiful thing. It produces perseverance. Adversity is all part of God's plan to develop our understanding of true love.

Many of us have been taught that adversity was a result of the Fall, and if Adam and Eve had not sinned, we would never experience adversity of any kind. This is untrue. Adversity was created by God and is needed to build strength. The Bible says that even Jesus learned obedience through suffering. If Jesus was the Second Adam and was completely without sin, why would suffering teach Him anything? Everything in this world grows and is tested through adversity. Even trees become stronger through drought and storms. They need these things to develop deeper roots and stronger branches. Instead, we're to rejoice in our sufferings. Why? Because suffering produces perseverance. Everyone who is godly in Christ Jesus will suffer.

The whole reason love always perseveres is because of love's foundation. Understand that though perseverance is learned in life, it is immediate in love. The Bible doesn't say love learns to persevere; it simply says that love always perseveres. Just as love does not learn to be patient or kind, these things are immediate when love is present. The foundation of love is what makes them immediate. Unless the proper foundation is laid, love will never survive even the slightest breeze. The reason the world has taught us that perseverance is of minimal importance in love is because the world has also taught us either to lay no foundation at all or to lay a flimsy and worthless foundation.

When I was a singles pastor I found that the average amount of time a couple know each other before they have sexual intercourse is about two weeks. The problem with this is that sex ends up becoming the foundation of the relationship. Sex was never meant to be the foundation of a relationship. It was designed by God to be the consummation. The foundation of relationship is love.

God Always Perseveres

Had I not truly fallen in love with people, I would never have imagined that the foundation of love is what it is. Love's foundation is downright intimidating to people who don't love. It's more than a mystery; it's repulsive. Believe it or not, the foundation of love is actually death. If you die to yourself, you can endure anything in your relationship. The power of endurance and perseverance comes alive when you are in it for someone else. Perseverance in love is for the sake of the other person, not for your sake. The only way to possess it is if the relationship is not about you. The final test of perseverance is really a test to see if you are in it for you or for others.

In the weight-lifting world there is a saying: "No pain, no gain." In the world of relationships a similar saying might be: "No death, no life." Until the foundation of death is laid, love will have no perseverance and will surely fail the test. It can have every single ingredient to it that we have talked about in the previous chapters, but until a person is dead to him- or herself, it is *not* love. Love will be tested because love is not satisfied with illustrations of its power and genuineness. Love requires demonstrations.

Jesus gave illustration after illustration of what love is, and then at the end of His life, He gave us the greatest demonstration of love the world has ever seen. It was the final thing that had to happen to prove that what He said and did was authentic. Christ is a perfect picture of love's foundation.

He is the essence of it. Authentic relationship cannot even begin until death to self takes place. This is why Jesus told us to "take up" our crosses, and "Whoever desires to save his life will lose it, but whoever loses his life for My sake will find it." This truth holds the key to how life works.

There is a curious verse in the last book of the Bible that says, "The Lamb [was] slain from the foundation of the world." This has bewildered theologians for years because it seems to be saying that the sacrifice we humans witnessed two thousand years ago was merely a snapshot of what had already taken place before the beginning of time. Even Old Testament verses in Isaiah that talk of the Messiah speak in past tense as though the sacrifice had already happened. Many theologians say that the reason it took place before the foundation of the world was because God knew ahead of time that man would sin.

After coming to know His heart, however, I believe this analysis is only half right. I believe that the sacrifice took place at the foundation of the world because God desired relationship, and that is what is required: death to self. Later, when man sinned and needed atonement, the sacrifice that had already taken place in heaven simply manifested itself here on earth. I've come to believe that even if Adam and Eve were never going to sin, the "Lamb" would still have been slain at the foundation of the world. Relationship demands it. Death to self is the essence of heart connection, and this was what God was aiming for when He created you and me.

Self-death covers everything a relationship may need in the future. It is what makes perseverance instantaneous in love. Adam and Eve were covered long before they were formed out of clay and given life. Their Father told them the same thing I told my children even before they were born: that no matter what happened, I would never leave them. I would die for them. And with us, God ensured it by giving Himself up for us from the very start. Christ's death not only atoned for our sin, but it proved His love. And as we've seen, love is not complete until it's shown to persevere through testing. To accomplish His purpose and reveal the Father's heart to the world, Jesus had to show us that He'd die so we could live.

Because of this, there is no doubt that God will persevere with you for all eternity. He has already given up Himself for you. Think about it. Living in the heart of the ones you love can happen only if you die to yourself. Until you do, people will always remain a mystery to you. Men will never understand their wives and women will never understand their husbands until they stop living for themselves and start living for the other person. Death (that is, self-sacrifice) is the very foundation of every true relationship in the world. Until you give up your life, you will never find it. Think about the message Jesus preached throughout His entire ministry: "Give up your life" and "Greater love has no one than this, that he lay down his life for his friends." And the apostle Paul said, "It is no longer I who live, but Christ lives in me."

Because we downplay and diminish the significance of perseverance in today's society, we also minimize it when it comes to God's heart. This is why it's so easy for people to imply that God might be getting to a boiling point with the world today. It's why so many of us believe that He just might wash His hands and give up on us.

This view of God's heart has influenced countless Christians. Some people honestly believe that they have gone from saved to unsaved and back to saved again numerous times in their lives. They don't believe for a minute that God's love for them perseveres because they haven't embraced the sacrifice of Christ fully in their hearts.

Many beautiful things happened between God and us as a result of the death and resurrection of Christ. Unfortunately, most of those things are disregarded in today's theology. We have become so ensnared by the Old Testament understanding of God that we have patterned our teachings and doctrines after it and have denied the wonderful new freedom available to us today.

Everything from Bible reading to church attendance to the way we pray has been affected by Old Testament thinking. Popular teachings on worship, generational curses, fasting, tithing, receiving blessings, and even hearing the voice of God have all been poisoned by our lack of accepting and standing upon the substitution of Christ's death in place of anything we could ever do.

The purpose of the Old Testament is to point the way to Christ. For some reason, however, the church continues to run back to the Old Testament principles and deny the changes Christ brought about. They prefer to embrace the comfortable rules of religion rather than the confusing, difficult freedom of relationship.

We have become no different than the Jews who rejected Christ two thousand years ago. Accepting Christ does not mean that we accept the historical person of Christ only. It means that we accept everything He did and accomplished through His death and resurrection as well. When we routinely act and behave as though the Cross has provided nothing of any value, we are literally giving ourselves over to an anti-Christ spirit. We are denying the work that Christ did on the Cross. We must be willing to believe, receive, and live within that freedom of relationship He purchased for us.

The way we know the truth about God's limitless perseverance is when we accept grace and leave law-minded thinking. If you accept that He died for you, it changes everything. God is perseverance! He went through the fire and was found blameless, perfect! He paid ahead of time for all your sins. So don't ever worry that His endurance is running thin. The foundation of God's love for you is death, and love that is dead to self always perseveres!

CHAPTER 18

His Love Never Fails

When I first became a Christian, I had read just about every book on the market that dealt with spiritual warfare. These things fascinated me, so I immersed myself in the thousands of teachings on "casting out demons" and healing the sick.

David and Trisha, a young married couple, approached me about a young woman who was staying with them. They told me that they were sure she was demon-possessed. They asked me if I would be willing to stop by their apartment after work and minister to her. Immediately, my heart began to pound with a combination of fear and excitement. Everything I had studied for so long was about to be put to the test.

After agreeing to help, I began praying in the kitchen of the restaurant I was working in. I had about forty-five minutes until I got off work, so I had to make the best of my time. Just as I was doing "faith exercises" and searching the cupboards for olive oil with which to perform an anointing, David walked into the kitchen and informed me that he and his wife were going out of town. I would be all alone with this demonic woman. Now I went from fear and excitement to plain fear.

In the next forty minutes, I prayed every spiritual warfare prayer I had ever learned. I was speaking in tongues so fast, I think even God needed an interpretation. I left work early and drove around their block seven times, "claiming it" for God. Just before I knocked on the door, I put a little anointing oil on my fingers, hoping to shake her hand and surprise the demons. My heart was racing as I waited for her to answer the door.

Slowly, the doorknob began to turn as if a child were behind it, trying to work it open. Then the door quietly opened to just a crack and stopped. I could see her peeking at me. "Are you the pastor?"

I had never been called "Pastor" before, so I didn't really know what she meant. But I knew she was expecting me, so I said, "Yes, I am." After allowing me inside, I could see she was terrified. *It must be God she sees in me*, I thought to myself. I held out my oil-soaked hand like a spiritual bear trap on the end of my wrist and tried to get her to shake it. When she shook my hand, to my amazement, nothing happened! No shrieks or screams, no split pea soup or uncontrollable growling. Nothing!

I wondered if she might not be demon-possessed after all. Her unresponsiveness to my anointing-oil handshake was a dead giveaway. I asked her what the problem was, and she began to tell me about a demon that lived in her who spoke to her all the time. She even told me his name. I asked her if I could pray with her, and she consented with one stipulation: I wasn't allowed to use the "J-word," *Jesus.*

But that was paralyzing! It was like training a soldier in the use of a weapon and then stripping him of it moments before battle. How in the world was I supposed to cast this demon out without using the name of Jesus? Everything I had learned up to this point hinged on my using that name. Without it, I was useless.

Over the next hour and a half, I launched every spiri-

tual warfare tactic I'd learned in the preceding six months.
I "pleaded the blood," rebuked the demon, and called down
the blessings, but nothing happened. I was dead in the water.
I truly felt like a traveling snake-oil salesman at the end of
his bag of tricks.

After sitting with her for more than two hours and,
frankly, feeling embarrassed and a bit faithless, I was perplexed and emotionally spent. While I sat there trying to
remember another technique, I caught a glimpse of this poor
little girl sitting in front of me. She hadn't slept in days. I saw
this precious girl so wrapped up in fear she could barely sit
still. All at once, my heart began to break for her, almost as if
she were my own child. I walked across the room, took her in
my arms, and held her tightly. Everything inside me melted,
and I cried with her as we held each other.

That moment, this wonderful girl was set free. Her name
was Joy, and she had reclaimed her joy in my arms. I learned
that day that tricks are for kids. Though I was stripped of
using Jesus' name, I found that if I *became* Jesus to her, all the
power of the universe was at my fingertips. It was love that set
her free. From that day forward, my entire ministry has been
built on that foundational truth. God is love. Nothing can
stand up to that. Nothing.

Because we have so many different definitions of love, it's
sometimes difficult to know exactly what the Bible means
when it says to "love" people. We say we love pizza and we tell
our spouses we love them too. Where does the love of God fit
in? Somewhere between a pizza and a wife?

If you have ever been "in love," you'll agree there's nothing like it in the world. It consumes your entire being. Your
whole life is about that person. You literally meditate on them
night and day. Everything you do is for them. It's as though

you've taken that person into your heart and spirit, and you see deeper inside them than anyone else on the planet. There is truly nothing in the world like it.

Though being "in love" consumes every part of our souls, many of us have developed a fear of it. Being completely drained by love can be terrifying. We've come to believe being in love once or twice in a lifetime is about all a person can handle. After that, you simply cannot take any more.

This might scare you, but the love of God is not somewhere between a pizza and our spouses. In fact, the love of God *is* being "in love." The love of God literally *is* being head over heels in love with people. There is no middle ground in loving people when it comes to loving God. The only way to fulfill the teachings of Jesus is to be head over heels in love with others. Everything He said to do in regard to others is the very thing that people who are in love do naturally. It takes being in love to accomplish the many aspects of love described in this book. There is simply no way to do these things unless you are in love.

And that might appear a bit disheartening. It may even seem impossible. Wouldn't our hearts explode with that much love?

When my wife was pregnant with our second child, I was both excited and concerned. I was concerned because I couldn't fathom loving this child as much as I already loved my first. I'd already given every part of my father heart to Landin. She was my world. There simply wasn't anything left of me to give. I felt like I would have to take away some of my love for Landin in order to have something to give to Sidney, and that wasn't an option.

Then one day, when Sidney was a week old, I was holding her in my arms and out of the blue our eyes met and she smiled at me. That little smile pierced straight through my silly fears. Instantly an explosion of love flooded my soul, and an entire new universe of Sidney forced its way into my heart. In a matter of weeks, I found that there were parts of me I didn't even know existed. I became so in love with Sidney that I could hardly stand it. From that day until the present, Sidney has remained in the center of her daddy's heart.

By the time Emma, Eva, and Jude came along, I wasn't worried in the least. I had already learned the most beautiful lesson of life. I learned that the capacity for love in our human hearts is limitless. There's literally no end to how much love one person can possess for others. Believe it or not, I could have a thousand children and be head over heels in love with each and every one of them.

If God is love and love comes from God, believing we could ever run out of love is simply shallow thinking. The problem is, just like when I visited Joy, we have to want to possess love. Unfortunately, I've found that most Christians aren't moved by this truth. Most people just aren't interested in doing this. It's not appealing. Not only does it sound incredibly difficult, there doesn't seem to be any real personal benefit. Ironically, this is why many people become saturated with the practices of religion. It becomes a way to bypass love and preoccupy ourselves with the pretty-colored rules and regulations. We spend more time trying to perform the effects of love than we do loving.

Too many of us spend our time memorizing Scriptures, using Jesus' name, and claiming promises in an effort to get ahold of God's power. Some people follow big-name evangelists around the country, hoping God's power will rub off on them. There are books, tape series, and conferences that are specifically designed to show people how to access God's power. Supernatural power has become the most desired commodity instead of love. But God never told us to seek His power. He told us to seek Him. The Bible doesn't say "God is power." It says God is love.

Here's the truth: either we can have faith to access the power of God or we can have love and *become* the power of God. Faith is important, but faith without love is useless. You can bind demons, tear down "spiritual strongholds," and even move mountains, but if you don't love, you're wasting your time. No amount of spiritual armor, anointing oil, or seed-faith offerings will ever take the place of love. All these things are wonderful, but remember this: if you love, you will have God's power automatically! Love *is* the power of God. It is the fulfillment of every word in Scripture. Love is not just one of many things a Christian should practice; it is *everything!*

A person may not be a Christian, but if she truly loves people, she has more of God's power than a Christian who doesn't love. Love is unstoppable. It topples everything in its path. And all of God's power resides in your love for people. When you love someone, you're literally putting the power of the universe inside your heart. Nothing can withstand it.

This love didn't detonate in my life until I understood and believed that God loved me this way. When I finally got it and *knew that I knew* that God was crazy about me for no other reason than that I was His son, I began to love others. I was no longer fulfilling an obligation or meeting a quota. Because He loved me and I knew it, I could just relax and experience that love by pouring it into others. Receiving the truth of His love for you is the starting point. That will cut through everything and penetrate your heart because love never fails.

When the Bible says if you live in God, He will live in you, that's referring directly to love. There's no other way to live inside someone. God is telling you that He not only loves you, but also He's "in love" with you. He is head over heels in love with *you*! But you have to receive that love from Him if you want to become a lover of others.

How to Make It Work

From the time I was a little boy attending our family church in Phoenix, Arizona, I've heard no less than a thousand different teachings on how to know God's heart. Some say that to know the Bible is to know God. Others teach that knowing Him comes only through hours of dedicated prayer time. Theologians look for Him in the original Greek and Hebrew texts of the Scriptures. And pastors tell us He speaks through every sermon they preach. I've heard that I could find Him through passionate worship, generous giving, and tireless works. It's been said that if we follow the laws of God, we will know His heart. Knowing His heart has been the quest of every well-meaning Christian from even before the time Jesus walked the earth.

Not only do we wish to know His heart, but we also long to hear His voice. We want to know when He speaks to us, and what He's saying. This desire to know and hear Him is built into every human heart. It springs from our sincere and unalterable need for true relationship with our Creator.

The grievous fact about this generation is not the lack of desire to know His heart, but how little we know of Him despite our desire to do so. It crushes me to see sincere people run through the spiritual obstacle courses of religion in an effort to get close to God, only to end up as lost as they were before. And what's even worse is that every year a new batch of teachings comes along and adds to the confusion.

This is why Christianity has become a religion of stalkers.

We read about God in the Bible, we analyze His works, and we memorize stories about Him. And then we think we know Him. We witness to people about this guy we read about in a book who supposedly saved us from something, but we have no idea who or what or why. Sadly, most Christians today seem to know about God, but they don't know Him. This is exactly what stalkers do.

I could talk until I'm blue in the face, but until you know the people in my heart, you will never know me. The people in there are me, and I am them. If you give one of them something, you give it to me. If you steal from one of them, you are stealing from me. If you're their friend, you're mine. There's simply no way to know my heart other than by knowing theirs. There's no way to touch my heart without going through them.

I have people who have dedicated their entire lives to supporting me and the causes I stand for. They stand up for me, they give their money, and they donate their time. These people *are* my heart. They're precious, and I love them more than they will ever know. But if they didn't know the people in my heart—my wife and kids—they wouldn't know my heart. I wouldn't be upset with them over it. It's just a fact. If they didn't know them, they wouldn't know me.

There are also people I know who don't lift a finger for me. They're not involved in my life, they don't partner with me in my ministry, and they haven't read any of my books or listened to a single sermon of mine in their entire lives. But they're centered on knowing and loving my family, and because of this, these people know me, they know my heart, and they minister to me. They know me better than the ones who spend all their time with me.

I know pastors who spend six hours a day reading and studying their Bibles. The pages look like they've been through battle. And they have. Everything is underlined and highlighted. There are notes scribbled in all the margins, and key words are circled on every line. They spend hours every day in their prayer closets crying out to God. But when it comes to people, they're indifferent. They could take them or leave them. These men think they know God's heart because they've read and studied His Book and spent hours in prayer, but what they don't know is that they're being grossly deceived. They don't know Him from Adam!

I also know people who read their Bibles about five minutes a week and pray even less. They secretly kick themselves for it, and they're afraid to approach God because their religion has made them so aware of their sin. However, they happen to love people with all their hearts. These folks have an intimacy with God that's irreplaceable. They know Him fully because they love and know His children.

There is no question in my mind that in the end there will be millions who thought they knew Him, but didn't, and trillions who were convinced they didn't know Him, but really did.

CHAPTER 19

Touching God

A while ago, I came home early from work. I wasn't feeling great, and as I was lying on the couch, my daughter Sidney was sitting on our reclining chair next to me, watching *Barney & Friends*. As I was about to relocate myself to another part of the house to preserve my remaining sanity, my eyes fell on my precious daughter. She was completely entranced. Her eyes were wide with wonder, and her face was shining. She didn't know I was watching her; in fact, she didn't even know I was in the room at that point, so I took full advantage of the opportunity. I found myself gazing at her for a long time.

My entire world was sitting on a reclining chair watching a big purple dinosaur. She was the most precious person I'd ever known. Before long I was warm all over and started to get choked up. I admired every line of her face. Her enormous brown eyes and cute, pudgy nose. Even her fingers moved my heart, so small and perfect. And my favorite feature, her precious little lips, like a miniature of her mother's.

Standing there, I realized that inside me, there is a flame of love for that little girl that burns in my chest. It's a different color for each of my children, and it started with my wife long before they were born. For the last several years, that flame has grown to an internal forest fire. Sometimes it literally takes my breath away when one of them walks into the room and smiles at me. My entire life is guided by that flame.

So here is the point we've been coming to all along. It's very simple, yet incredibly profound. Wise men can't understand it, but as little children they were all born understanding it. This one truth has completely changed my life:

> When you truly love someone unconditionally with all that's in you, that flame of love inside your heart is God.

And the most freeing fact you could ever learn is that you don't need to look for Him anywhere else. He's not somewhere up in the sky or far off on a mountaintop. He isn't traveling with an evangelist, waiting for you to show up to the service. He isn't sitting in your church, waiting for you to get out of your seat and join the club. When you love, He is already living inside you!

God. *Is*. Love.

I've watched thousands of people over the years desperately search for the "fire of God" in prayer meetings, conferences, and worship services. They scream at the top of their lungs and fall on the ground waiting for it to hit them. It's been preached about from every pulpit in America and all the while, it existed in the hearts of people who love. The fire of God *is* love!

All the answers in the universe are found in that flame of love inside your heart. If you analyze that flame, you will find all wisdom and grace; you will possess supernatural understanding and untainted spiritual insight. You will not need anyone to teach you because His Spirit will lead you into all truth.

I have watched parents cry out to God for wisdom in rearing their children. They have lost sight of what to do next. They beg God to lead them to a Scripture or a Christian book that will give them the answers they seek.

God's response goes something like this: "Consult the flame."

If you look to that flame of love you have in your heart for your child and consult it, you will know how to act and react. Try it. Discipline will become precise and godly every time. The flame reveals the inner parts of your child's heart to you. It shows you exactly what to do in every situation. The problems come because most of us get angry and frustrated and we hide from it. We forget that we love our children. The moment we do this, we become instantly deaf, dumb, and blind. Then we need a Bible verse or a book to bail us out. But if we keep our eyes on the flame, all the answers will come.

I will never forget the day my daughter Landin was running around the hotel we were staying in the night before we went to Disneyland. She was so excited she could hardly contain herself. Without thinking, she ran by her sister and slapped her on the back as hard as she could. Sidney immediately broke out in a level-eight cry. I grabbed Landin and looked into her eyes. "What are you thinking?" I shouted in total disbelief. My eyes were those of a father who had no idea who his child was. What I saw as my precious little daughter drank in that look was unforgettable. Her spirit deflated and her heart broke right in front of me. Immediately, the flame singed my conscience and showed me the pain I'd just caused her with that look. Right away, I took her in my arms. "Daddy knows you didn't mean to hit Sidney. You were just excited, weren't you? I understand. But you can't hit her, even when you're excited, okay?"

The flame not only convicted me, it gave me the exact words to make it right. It showed me a clear picture of what had happened and an instant blueprint on how to fix it. Religion is the rule book that teaches you to say, "I'm sorry." But the flame gives you the heart of truth that hits the mark every time. All the answers to parenthood are found in the flame because God is the flame. God is love.

Husbands and wives pray for wisdom in their marriages. They struggle to the point of divorce because nothing comes. God's response: "Consult the flame." Look at that spouse you loved so much and remember. Search your heart for that flame that used to burn so hot it made you feel sick. Find it. And then consult it! Understanding is found in that flame. Grace lives there. Marriage counseling is for people who blew the flame out and either refuse to relight it or think they've forgotten how. But if they would simply embrace the flame of love inside, there's nothing their marriages could not overcome.

Christians tell me every day of the week that reading the Bible has become mundane and boring for them. They've tried switching translations in an effort to mix the words up a bit, but eventually they find themselves right back where they started. God's response to this one is also to consult the flame. All Scripture must be seen in the light of the flame. Without it, it will be dark in your hands. It's not the Bible that makes the flame come to life; it's the flame that makes the Bible come to life. The Bible must be seen through the flame, or its beauty, life, instruction, and hope will be invisible to you.

The Bible is a revelation of God's heart, a revelation of love. The flame is "the Word" living inside you! The entire Bible already exists within the flame that is alive inside your heart. If you have to run to your Bible for an answer, it's because you've forgotten the flame.

All of Christianity must be seen through the flame of love. Our entire faith is based on it. Every aspect of God's character is revealed in that flame as well. His desires, His tone, and His countenance can be known only in the flame.

That flame gives me boldness to speak the truth regardless of the consequences. It kindles a desire in me to set people free and bring them to liberty at any cost. No opposition will come against me that's stronger than my love for people. My family and I have undergone unimaginable persecution because of this message. I've been blackballed from entire ministries and rejected by friends and colleagues. Lies have been told about me, and my words are endlessly misquoted and taken out of context. And all in an effort to destroy my credibility and suffocate these words.

When you become acquainted with that flame and you know Him well, and you trust the flame to guide you and lead you into all truth, you'll be able to say, "I have been to the Father, and I speak only what I've seen and what He tells me. I have seen Him and touched Him," in the same way Jesus said it. After a lifetime of consulting the flame of love within my heart, I have found some of the most beautiful truths I could have ever imagined.

I found that:

God is incredibly patient. He understands everything in your heart. He knows why you do what you do, and He is never surprised or caught off guard. God is kind, and He wants you to feel His touch in your heart, that heart He created to long for Him, for love.

God never envies anyone or anything. He never desires to take for Himself what others have. Instead, He longs to give away all He has, and He's never tempted to take things back because He didn't get enough attention. God doesn't boast about the highest truths about Himself; He willingly lowers Himself even lower than you just to lift you up. God is not proud, holding to His perfection and reminding us He doesn't need anyone. He desires a relationship with you and me, and He continually makes Himself vulnerable just to make that possible.

God is *never* rude. He doesn't leave anything unfinished or unspoken. He is incapable of giving anyone "the silent treatment" or playing hide-and-seek when they're earnestly seeking Him. He makes everything about Himself known and has no desire to keep anything hidden from you.

God cannot be self-seeking. He is gratified and fulfilled when *you* are praised and honored. His eyes are always seeking the best for you, and He's never worried about what He gets in return. He isn't provoked easily or ever angered beyond His desire for complete love. He's not "high maintenance," and He never wants you to walk in fear of offending or hurting Him. He keeps no record of the wrong things you've done because He refuses to call you by the name of your past. He doesn't hold anything over your head, but continuously wipes your record clean so that He can clearly focus on your heart.

God doesn't delight in evil, and He's never tempted to follow lies and fantasies. He doesn't desire romantic notions, just the real you. He can't countenance anything that would benefit His kingdom at your expense. He rejoices in the truth about you because He sees who you truly are and it's beyond wonderful to Him. God always protects you from caving in to pressure, despair, or anguish. If you'll simply ask Him, He will always provide the strength needed to hold you up through the storms of life and *carry* you in His own strong arms to your intended purpose as His favorite, irreplaceable child.

God always trusts you, with His heart doors open at all times, without exception. He always hopes in you because He knows the endless truth of your never-ending story. God always perseveres, proving He is who He claims to be. He stands through the storm and walks through the fire simply to express His love for you. He will never fail you, never fall short, never fall out of love, because He's made of love, the very source of it all.

Love is why He sees everything inside you and knows every emotion, thought, and feeling. Love is why He soaks through every outward thing that stands in the way to saturate your spirit, soul, and heart with the knowledge of blissful eternity with Him. Love is why there's no place, no person, and no created thing that can be separate from Him.

He is all-knowing, all-powerful, all wonderful.

He. *Is*. Love.

Acknowledgments

I would like to acknowledge the original group who experienced this magical truth as it was unfolded to us in the choir room many years ago. Though we called ourselves many names ("Shiloh," "Night Light," "Saturday Night Live"), we were just a group of hurting people who were courageous enough to open our hearts to the unimaginable. Together we became castaways and criminals forced to go underground with the greatest revelation we'd ever known. I swore to you in the beginning that this message would be worth it. May it go to the ends of the earth now.

Though the truth of Love was in existence before the world was created, it will always feel to us that it's "our message."

Coming soon from *Windblown Media*

windblown
MEDIA
Newbury Park, California

Also from Windblown Media

windblown
MEDIA
Newbury Park, California

He Loves Me: Learning to Live in the Father's Affection
by Wayne Jacobsen

If your spiritual life feels more like an empty ritual rather than a joyful journey, let Wayne help you discover this Father who loves you more than anyone on this planet ever has or ever will, and how you can rest in his love through every circumstance you face.

So You Don't Want to go to Church Anymore by Wayne Jacobsen and Dave Coleman

Frustrated pastor Jake Colsen meets a man who talks about Jesus like no one he's ever met. Could this be one of Jesus' original disciples still alive in the twenty-first century, and should he believe the crazy way he talks about life, faith, and community?

The Shack by Wm. Paul Young

Mackenzie Allen Philips's youngest daughter, Missy, has been abducted during a family vacation and evidence that she may have been brutally murdered is found in an abandoned shack deep in the Oregon wilderness. Four years later, in the midst of his *Great Sadness*, Mack receives a suspicious note, apparently from God, inviting him back to that shack for a weekend. Against his better judgment he arrives at the shack on a wintry afternoon and walks back into his darkest nightmare. What he finds there will change Mack's world forever. Here's what Eugene Peterson, translator of *The Message*, said about this book:

"When the imagination of a writer and the passion of a theologian cross-fertilize, the result is a novel on the order of The Shack. *This book has the potential to do for our generation what John Bunyan's* Pilgrim's Progress *did for his. It's that good!"*

My Beautiful One Instrumental CD

Seldom do songs transcend the realm of words and touch your spirit, but this one does. This music will capture you, restore your soul, and draw you near to the very heart of God. What *The Shack* did with words, Chris DuPré does with music. That's why we are proud to release *My Beautiful One* as our debut album for Windblown Records—a definite "must hear."

Compelling stories that unveil God's heart to the spiritually curious
www.windblownmedia.com
(805) 498-2484